Mastering Badassery
With
Truth

By
Daune Thompson

Published by I Deserve It Consulting, LLC
Copyright © 2023 by Daune Thompson

ISBN: 979-8-218-33232-7

IDI Coaching does not dispense medical advice or prescribe the use of any technique as a form of treatment for physical or medical problems without the advice of a physician, either directly or indirectly. The intent of IDI Coaching/Training is only to offer information of a general nature to help you in your quest for emotional and spiritual well-being. If you use IDI Coaching principles for yourself, the owners of IDI Coaching (Open Mind Consulting) assume no responsibility for your actions.

All rights reserved. No part of this book may be reproduced in any form or by any means without the author's or publisher's prior written consent.

Edited by R. Jill Maxwell
Rjillmaxwell.com - Scottsdale, AZ

Also, by Daune Thompson

∞

I Deserve It Dream Book
Kids Only

I Deserve It Dream Book
Adults Edition

Drama Detox
Stop Self-Sabotage Before It Stops You

Balls
Building Balanced Relationships

idi Meditation Journal
Meditation and Journaling in One

I Deserve It
Events and Retreats

I Deserve It Products
Truth Apparel

For information about bulk purchases of this book
or other **idi** materials,
please get in touch with Daune Thompson at:

www.ideserveitnow.com
www.daunethompson.com
info@ideserveitnow.com

DEDICATION

This book is dedicated to my husband, Tony, who has never wavered as my biggest supporter. He stood strong when I questioned if TRUTH was worth it and pushed me directly into it.

CONTENTS

1. Who's the Boss of You?
2. Expecting Wounded Souls to Save Us
3. No More Effing Rules
4. Drama Stew
5. Pain Is Your Internal Healer
6. Are You Answering The Yeti?
7. Awakening is a Choice, Not an Event
8. Low Vibe Emotions
9. Licking The Curb For Love
10. Neutral Isn't Nice - It's Nothing
11. Sugarcoating and Adversity
12. Are the Signs Really Everywhere?
13. Intentionally Burning Intentions?
14. Truth Consciousness
15. Observing Yourself Experiencing
16. Rat Race Realization
17. Relationships Are Revealing You
18. Astrology Lost It's Woo Woo

19. Does the "F" Word Upset You?
20. Power Tools Come in Many Forms
21. Your Parents' Marriage Mirage
22. Truth Trumps Trash
23. God Glow
24. Labels Limit So Lose Them

INTRODUCTION

Definition: A badass is someone who does the dirty jobs, the jobs that other people do not want to do. A badass does what needs to be done, no matter how difficult it is, without complaint or need for fanfare. A badass doesn't take the path of least resistance.

Definition: *bad*: unacceptable, wrong, poor, inadequate, unacceptable. It's the act of disrupting an established order, so it fails to continue.

Definition: *ass*: stubbornness or disobedience of a donkey. Let's keep it simple and use stubborn ass.

Badass is an image of an individual who is in their power and doesn't fall prey to others' realities but lives authentically in their own power. They exude the confidence to live without stubbornly holding onto external establishments of thought. They are their own light. Mastering that light means mastering their own badassery.

Badassery is not a character flaw to overcome but a spiritual awakening of stepping into your power of authentic truth.

No one directed me toward the truth or offered an alternative path. The struggle of not fitting in became the catalyst for finding a better way. I had to navigate and show myself a different route.

I remember adults dictating that their way was better: "just listen to us." However, this prescribed "better way" seemed utterly nonsensical. I'm here to tell you it doesn't have to be this difficult.

This is not a self-help book teaching you how to get out of your own bullshit. This book shows you where to look to see your bullshit, and let it go so you can live an authentic and truthful life.

Self-help is when you actually own your crap. Self-awareness is seeing it. Self-enlightenment is putting light into all the dark places you've avoided in exchange for becoming whole and complete in your truth.

I'm not here to motivate you. I'm disinterested in whiners. I'm not interested in your beliefs or bad habits either. I want you to see yourself. I am focused on directing your mind to know that you have the power to flip on the switch of your spiritual, mental, and physical DNA at any moment or all the time.

For most of my life, I have been able to see the truth that most people cannot see. Maybe they didn't want to see it. It didn't matter if I used feelings, observations, a blueprint energy tattoo, astrology, or a paper map to show others visually. The truth was always present, like a visual strobe light. Yet, it tripped me up every time I was told I wasn't smart enough, I wasn't good enough, I wasn't lovable enough, I wasn't what other people wanted me to be, because I couldn't live their sugar-coated life, or non-truth. This alienated many people when I spoke my truth, because I was the eternal doormat until I realized enough was enough and chose truth instead.

My goal with a truth book is to help you go inside yourself, look at all the rooms that are still dark in your lighthouse, and have enough courage to flip the switch and see that you are more than enough. You are superhuman, super light, and super powerful. My intention is and always will be to show you your gifts and why you sabotage yourself into doormat behavior by simply forgetting to look at yourself.

I hope you will see your truth or start questioning the truth and non-truths in your own life and not others. I wish for you to have the courage to stand as the brightest lighthouse on the block for those trying to find their way out of the stormy sea.

Now, I know what many of you might be thinking: your truth is the truth you follow, and that's all that matters. You're correct as long as that truth is you being the most loving, kind, compassionate, expanded, healthy, and confident person you can be. You will trip and fall if you demand others to change and accept your truth. If you can't be honest with yourself and see the bullshit that you drag to every person, place, and experience as your excuse to play small, this is not likely the book for you. You're not ready to see a truth that may trip up your entire reality as it is right now.

You were probably drawn to read this book because you are stuck. But let's be clear. Feeling stuck is not because you are not powerful. You are stuck because no one told you where to look so you could remove the boulders in your life and get on your brightest path. That path is to complete the karma you came to this earth to complete.

Karma means 'Doing' from the root word 'kri' - to do. Your thoughts about things become a reality. Are your current thoughts the things you want in your life?

IT'S TIME TO COMPLETE YOUR KARMA!

What do you need to do to complete your karmic lesson?

Look at the dark rooms in your reality and see yourself as a lighthouse with a few rooms still in the dark. You are a spark of light from source consciousness, and that spark of light resides in the heart. Your energy has shifted, and now you seek your inner truth, questioning yourself.

Perhaps you're a homemaker on the brink of divorce, a CEO realizing the absence of love and connection amidst financial success, an athlete no longer engaged in sports, a doctor witnessing a decline in healing abilities, a teacher lacking the ability to inspire students, or a young adult trapped in a career path that brings misery. The key concept here is realizing where you feel miserable.

If you're constantly busy, resistant to change, and set in your ways, eventually you'll experience pain in some aspect of your life that will expose these traits. A peaceful state is a natural easy way of living when you choose God consciousness inside you. The center is God's frequency or God's spark of light right down your spine in your DNA. So, it's highly likely your inner warrior spirit is testing you to listen to your heart instead of old past beliefs.

My simple explanation of a badass: *stubborn rule breaker*. Determined, living life to the fullest, leveling up, raising the bar, living on your terms, and living the life you deserve.

That is the description of badass. However, you choose to hear what you want: bad words or stubborn rule-breakers. You decide.

This book will ask you to step into being a stubborn rule-breaker. Enter with intention.

Wishing you the life you truly Deserve,
Love, Daune

HOW TO USE THIS BOOK

We were often told not to write in our books as young children. You've heard it: "Don't get it dirty. Keep it clean." This is a little different.

This is your book. Get it dirty. Write all over it. Use the Journal Spot in the back to write down in your own words what you want to remember and incorporate into your life. I encourage you to underline the areas that make you wonder. Write out questions that come up. Draw pictures to get you thinking of possibilities. Pay special attention to answering or addressing the exercise questions provided at the end of each chapter. They'll help you by guiding your thoughts toward embracing Badassery in your life.

Lastly, here is a full disclosure and a simple reminder for everyone who reads this book: this is Mastering Badassery, not the sugarcoat-it tribe. I'm here to give you brutal truth in a safe place to look at yourself and ask, "Is this my truth?" or "If it was my truth, would it improve my life for the better if I open up to this new truth?" My purpose is to bring new, expanded thought to the planet, and it's up to each of us to integrate this expansion as it applies to us individually. Universal truths are much different than those of ego truths. So, cutting through all your BS is my ultimate goal! The truth is not easy to digest, but it is the fastest way to expand.

Don't skip to the end of each chapter, where you will find exercises to complete. Go ahead, break the old rules we've been taught, and write in this book! It's yours! Take action immediately! Pen to paper takes energy from your soul and activates it. If you listen to the audio, get a journal to write your answers.
Lastly, you may encounter a few colorful words in this reading. Please choose to see my passion ... I'm just being me and keeping it real.
Let's dig in.

1

Who's the Boss of You?

...

In my 30 years of teaching, I've observed one thing we ALL have in common: we've become victims of fear. We only share our fear in hushed corners and often follow with the words, "Don't tell anyone I'm afraid." We've lost all ability to speak our fears out to the world so we can then stop them from ravaging our realities. We've achieved very little understanding of what fear is and why it's so debilitating.

When fears and frustrations surface, that's our good old-fashioned Ego. You know that inner voice, which sounds like a monster or a beast, bullying and scaring the crap out of us. The ego has an important job: to keep us alive. The ego guards against any change that seems to threaten our existence, even if that change is best for us. Ego wants us to be so afraid that we don't go too wild and crazy about our big dreams. The ego promotes fears and frustrations from childhood traumas. This culprit throws a wrench in our evolution and growth, causing us to feel powerless and defeated. Now, what do we do?

Humans change for one of two reasons: choice or trauma. Typically, it's pain that forces us awake, unnerving as this may be. We wait until trauma knocks us on our asses, and then we all act stunned. What are we being awakened to? A choice to see the truth or not.

When we point fingers at others' undesired behaviors, we're outing ourselves of our inner fear or pain. We send accusations to deflect our wounds, but the pain still creeps in like a bully. This bully is good for us! Stay with me. Why would a surfacing fear be good for us? *The Answer*: Because it's easier to address pain we can see on the outside than it is locked hidden inside. "*Oh no!*" Ego screams. "*Don't tell anyone I have hurdles to overcome!*" That's how bullies work. They make you feel powerless so they can control you. Unless we intentionally choose to change a poorly taught belief, we won't likely make changes until a traumatic experience forces us past our secret fears.

Furthermore, we unknowingly accepted our minds being programmed with years of fear believing that people with "titles" (doctor, teacher, clergy, etc.) were qualified to be the bosses of us. Their "titles" determined our fate, which I've personally come to learn is total BS. This is happening to all of us now. We're finally asking ourselves who's programming our reality: us or someone else? Remember, we all fear something. What makes you or me different from anyone else on the planet experiencing the same fears? You stop accepting others' limited beliefs as your own!

External fearful experiences trigger a healing crisis in some areas of our lives. Avoiding and ignoring them is up to us. It separates the LEADERS from the followers, the SUCCESSFUL from the victims, and WINNERS from whiners. Fears are pre-programmed illusions. Fears make us feel like we have no control and then bully us into submission. This is NOT true! *You are* the boss of yourself, not the beast, nor the external "title" bullying you into things you know aren't in your highest good.

What can we learn when our fears surface? It's the Universe asking, "*What do you want?*"
And no cop-out answer of "*I don't know.*" We *do* know. We're just afraid to admit it. For example, when we choose what we want… are we upset when others don't resonate with our truth? Do we try to force our truth on others? Are we looking for others to decide our fate for us? Or are we just afraid to say, "*I want this…*" Then to hold firm in not allowing others' judgment to trigger our fears of rejection and doubt?

Listen to yourself! Do you hear how self-sacrificing and victim-mentality that is? Be the boss of you!

When we can't recognize our fears, they expose themselves as projections of anger and control and take on forms such as bullying, self-sacrificing, or simply magic pills to save us. It's time to look inside ourselves and ask, "*What am I afraid of?*" and "*If I'm the boss of me, what can I choose instead?*"

We're not being asked to change who we are at our core. Nor is our purpose or truth being challenged! It's our programmed fears up for grabs. Fear is each soul fighting to be free from societal norms that don't align with it. Look at the fear and ask, "*What would my life look like without (that fear)?*"

Remember, you are the boss of you. When I suggest people do what they want and not what they are expected to do, they often reply, "*I'm afraid of being rejected.*" Do it anyway! You'll appreciate how powerful it feels to be the boss of your fate afterward!

Please note: Sometimes, simply identifying and writing down our fears and reading them aloud is enough to expose and address them. Other times, they require more action.

EXERCISES

1. Write down one or two of your fears that keep reappearing.

2. Ask yourself what this fear would require you to see or acknowledge as your inner insecurities. Hidden insecurities that, at times, I project onto others, leading to unacknowledged blame for physical or emotional pain?

3. What word best describes the opposite of the pain you listed above?

BADASSERY EXTRA CREDIT TIP
Turn off your digital devices unless you are working.

2

Expecting Wounded Souls to Save Us

...

I want to start with a personal experience that I repeatedly see because we don't even realize when we're playing small and irresponsible.

I was on a business trip, and as I sat waiting for my flight, I overheard four adults discuss their grandkids and the mental challenges their grandkids were having. They shared about the shocking amount of medication a 12-year-old was on and how the doctor told his parents he was destined for a lifetime of Ritalin. Apparently, the doctor explained, he wouldn't get off it until he was 18 because his nerve synapses were not yet developed.

WOW! I was stunned that they were buying this BS! But I kept listening. Not one of them thought to challenge the doctor and ask, "Hey, how about instead we try incorporating personality education, self-esteem boosting techniques, or understanding nature's organic process?" The only option explained instead was a drug used to slow down mental capabilities and ruin his nervous system for a temporary fix. Six years of soul-numbing drugs for a child! This isn't healing; this is numbing and avoiding. It sounded to me like pouring Drano onto a wilting flower that just needed TLC, not more toxins.

The other couple involved in the conversation said they knew parents who'd sent their child away to every drug center and school possible to make their kid behave. The next man said their grandson got all the help imaginable, and he still lost his grandson to the streets because he wouldn't take his meds. These parents wanted a stranger to fix their kids' unhealthy love with numbing pills.

Let me be clear: ALL personality-altering medications are numbing some deeper wound or emotion(s) that parents refuse to face with their child or themselves. *(Countless research studies support this, but I will not get into it in this book. Do your own research if you dare.)*

Do some medications help in acute trauma and temporary situations, of course, but this isn't one of those very rare times. In this case, it's common to hear parents avoiding the responsibility of protecting their kids by saying NO to physicians! No more medications. Let's find another way. I choose nature." Until we detox the emotion and things that cause our internal pain, the pain will continue. No drug will solve it. Physically or emotionally. "No drug can save a negative person, and no poison can kill a positive person."

All I can say is "Hell yes!" to those kids for escaping the rules of Big Pharma, which uses parents to numb their kids with drugs instead of encouraging emotional exploration and expression. Not one of these grandparents mentioned that the parents of these kids were required to attend classes to unlearn any of their unhealthy habits, which clearly showed up in their children. Not one class was offered to unlearn unhealthy love and relearn healthy love. This simple truth alone has always blown my mind about why we are not seeking to learn healthy love instead of quick-fix pills.

Our kids have blueprints. We all do. If we don't understand that our kids' maps may be very different from our own, then, for God's sake, don't accept medication as the only option to numb their feelings. We must hear them out. We must learn about our own blueprints as well as theirs. Our jobs are to shine light, and kids are no different.

Believe it or not, our wounded kids or any relationships that challenge us right now are for our highest good to grow. They're the ones pressuring us to wake the hell up, not the other way around. A few of the lessons our children trigger in us:

- Are we holding on to familiar old stories that keep us in our comfort zone but do nothing for our growth or the growth of our children?
- Are we brutally honest with our internal crap?
- Do we expect other wounded souls who we don't know (i.e., TV wizards, commercials, doctors, etc.) to save us?
- How do we know if this healer, doctor, or teacher is also wounded or not?
- Do they enter the room as sunny solutions or as dangerous dark clouds?
- Are you grateful or groaning with another band-aid and no relief?

Relationships reveal our realities. This isn't only our kids and romantic love; it's all relationships. We must stop being nice to everyone, while standing in their projection of dark clouds on each of us, including people with titles and labels. It's time to take back our power.

Maybe we truly don't know who we are. Perhaps we've never considered self-assessment. It's time to ask ourselves better questions. Start today with a self-check such as: Am I the asshole or the awesome one?

Ask yourself: Do I judge, criticize, accuse, or do I recoil and fear others' behavior? Even those who I don't know?

If so, then you've swung out of a neutral state, and you are being pulled into their drama. What does that mean? It's not *our* job to determine if *they* are doing it right or wrong. Who gives a shit? What matters is that we know who we are here to be. Therefore, the only question that matters is, are we being it?

Are we truly being "THAT" person we want to be? Enough of this labeling people, "Oh, they're my soul mate/my family/my doctor of twenty years, my clergy…" They are energy, and we either fall for their dark drama or shine in their light. How's THAT for a reality check?

Until we each come to terms with God, the source, and our higher consciousness of love as our reality, we'll be in a constant duality of fighting truth with external illusion. Would God numb people's souls? You know the answer to that! If not, why the fuck are we?

Our souls were born in perfection. Now we're suffering through recycling trauma from our programmed illusions, or non-truths, all burning to the ground and crumbling. So, we are lost without instructions on how to proceed. This is the ego of duality versus the heart of God. The ego says, "I don't want to let go of my illusion of safety. I see this and that as good or bad, black or white, even if it's unhealthy." This illusion is comfortable for many but healing for none.

It's as simple as being awake or asleep. We don't question either of those. Your eyes are open or closed. Conscious means to be awake, or unconscious is the unseen and can get deluded.

So many are trying to make this a big conspiracy theory. "Well, they said this on the TV, so those TV wizards must be right." Brutal truth will tell us we have no fucking idea what someone else's truth is, or the truth traveling through millions of miles of cables connecting us to some studio, producing some words on a stage that another ego-driven person is reading. Is this a truthful reality or just one we've allowed?

It's time for us to acknowledge the temperature of our inner peace or our peace with God because religion is crumbling. God is not crumbling, but the indoctrination that God is out there and we're bad, which boxed religion teaches us, is crumbling. God is not out there. God is in our hearts when we live neutrally through our spines, hearts, and DNA (all of which come from God-sourced energy). We don't question what everyone tells us to question when we look inside ourselves instead.

- Should we be mad at anyone because they spoke the truth?
- Be mad because they chose happiness over anger?
- Should we be worried about losing our jobs because we are not following the norms and trends?
- If we put a purple, red, or black box on our social media, will we fit in with wizardry delusions?

I know this is still hard for many to hear, but the world is awakening, and it's simply a choice to be enlightened or stay in the dark. It's nothing more. The world has already shifted into the new earth frequency. It's up to each of us how we experience it. Are you going to be the pity or the party?

Can we walk out of our doors and know, without a doubt, that we're loving beings, whether someone is dressed as a unicorn, a clown, a lumberjack, a surfer, or in a pure white, pristine, conservative presentation, or everything in between? The only thing we should be asking is, "Am I being an asshole, or am I being an awesome soul?" Kindness wins, my friends, and it's felt, not merely seen. A simple solution to daily peace: Asshole or Awesome?

If we want happiness, it must come from our hearts. But if we're trying to tell someone how to live to make us happy, how *they* need to change to make *us* happy, how *they* did something that made *us* sad, then our hearts are not in charge. Our egos are. Our egos say, "To fit in, we're going to call people names until they do what we ask them to do. And, if we're mean enough, they'll lower their consciousness into my delusion of control."

Social media networks have programmed our delusions to tell us we have no power, so we don't have to think. My fellow humans, it's time to ask ourselves why do we listen to anyone or anything externally if God is in us?

We must allow everyone to live where they are. We also must love ourselves enough to stop accepting assholes telling us it's okay for them to behave angrily with us. So, *our litmus test is: am I an ASSHOLE or AWESOME?* This is so simple. When a TV wizard, friend, spouse, or neighbor comes to

tell us about their pity party, we must decide if this will be *our* future. None of it matters.
Because love wins.

Ever notice how being "happy" is feared, trashed, and condemned? Remember, misery loves company, and pity parties are a popular theme. It's up to each of us to stay LIT. If *we're in the* misery of the moment, it's time to ask ourselves why others are dropping out of our lives. Are we bright light energy, or are we Eeyore's?

Our relationships reveal our realities. Are we playing small or thriving? I can't stress this enough: our relationship with God will reveal our relationships with our external friends, family, lovers, and our relationship with ourselves. Are we connected to God or disconnected from God? The more disconnected we are, the angrier we get at those who don't give us what we want because they simply can't. No matter what we ask them for, expect disappointment. Who we are in our hearts is an inside job to decide.

I've got a challenge for us. Do we let wounded souls disconnect us from God? Do we allow others to determine our level of happiness and ability to thrive? If they're miserable (i.e., yelling, screaming, name-calling, and judging), do we allow them to pull us off our horses and stop our happy ride? If yes, WALK AWAY. This is a challenge for many.

Enough of the bullshit, enough of the virtue signaling, woke canceling, allowing others to tell us if we're going to be OK, and blaming others when we're not happy. *We* determine how our bubble of joy will look. If people are unkind, will you accept that behavior by saying, "Well, I just have to deal with it," or will you simply exit the environment? Again, this can be a job, friendship, marriage, family, or self-worth. This is how I choose to live my life, friends. I don't accept the "blame game" or "poor me" parties.

Will I react? No. Will I judge? No. I chose to be happy and thriving, empowered, and accountable. If it's not in my soul's power to live the same way, I will exit within thirty minutes of the heavy, weighted energy, grateful they're pushing me out. Whatever it takes, I will seek out light, find it, and never ask for permission again.

The Truth Tribe on my website is to help others understand we must stop asking for fucking permission to be happy. Our purpose is not what we're here to do as a career; it's who we want to be as a person. We need to stop defining our self-worth through a performance-based identity and the approval of others. What reality do we choose?

Try this: close your eyes, ask your heart, talk to your soul, and you'll find it's not that difficult to hear love consciousness in your heart. What do you love?

Depending on what we each want, how honest we are with where we are, and where we want to be, it takes the Universe to shift our frequencies from the old us to the new us. Letting go of our pity parties might be hard, at first, if the pity parties are habits. However, the sooner we make this shift, the happier our lives will be. Pity Party wounds appearing now are our pathway out. It's up to each of us to want to see them.

EXERCISES

1. Are you numbing or loving your emotions?

2. Are you grateful for pity party people delivering a litmus test to see if you are angry or loving? Are you the pity or the party?

3. How connected or disconnected to Source in your heart are you? Are you shining or dimming your lighthouse?

BADASSERY EXTRA CREDIT TIP

Litmus test yourself, are you an asshole or awesome? Do you take on drama and then fall into the pity party?

3

No More Effing Rules

...

Letting go of our rules about why we "can't" is where we'll break free. It's time to stop wasting our opportunities by adhering to other people's rules that do nothing for our growth. Wasting opportunities is a choice.

Rules we accept are the reality we choose. Nothing is an accident.

Until we become practiced in self-reviews, we'll feel like victims until we realize it's all our own doing. Our lives reflect our sonar sending out small, shady, victim behavior. Until we take a good look at our physical environments, our mental environments, and our spiritual environments, we're neglecting our own damn selves.

I also believe that when we're ready, we're ready. If we're distracting ourselves with external diversions or excuses, we aren't ready to invest in the root of the issue. The roots are the relief we seek, yet we refuse to do the work, dig further, and discipline ourselves to search for the deeper meaning of what's causing our pain. What's causing our pain are the "I Can" and "I Cant's" we learned as children. You know the words you heard often as a child, such as "You can't because you're different," "You can't because you're not old enough," "You can't because you're not pretty, smart, or capable of doing what they do." How about these timeless classics: "Rich people get rich off the backs of poor people," "Money doesn't grow on trees," or, the real BS story we all learned, "It's in your DNA, so you're going to get it, too."

We have become masters at avoiding our old, worn-out stories that shape our realities and prevent us from breaking the BS paradigms we've been taught. It's not even hard to identify the lessons we came to not only learn but also overcome. It's one of our personal roots, likely associated with our personal moon sign, which reveals where our shackles await release from the personal jail in which we decide to exist until one day, we don't. Like "poof!" This is no longer acceptable bullshit in your world. And you're done.

Many know the history of my personal development and coaching style. I use astrology natal birth maps to quickly validate an individual's gifts and remove challenges. This energy map simply reveals my clients' energetic tattoos. It's all of the energy we pass through as our souls choose to incarnate from source, through the galaxy and through planetary alignments giving us each an energy blueprint to follow. We chose that date and time to master those energy blocks in this lifetime? Yes, we each chose it. We brought a user's manual with us. So, don't avoid it.

I share this because it's unconventional and goes against the rules of healing in the typical mental health sciences, and many would say astrology is woo-woo and weird. Who taught us *those* rules? Because I know the validation I can offer clients is faster than therapy, I don't accept the norm for how to help each person take back his or her power. I delivered the same validation session whether they were CEOs, athletes, corporate executives, surgeons, accountants, healers, entrepreneurs, moms, or teens seeking to overcome bad habits. Following their validation sessions, they all had raving reviews of how well their personal tattoo revealed their answers within. Simple solutions we've all been told didn't exist. Is it unconventional? Yes, but seriously, enough of the fucking rules! If it works, why not open your mind to it? It seems like simple and quick would be more enjoyable than miserable and suffering. Just a thought.

Do we address all three aspects of ourselves (our bodies, minds, and spirits) when we're given an opportunity? A GO or green light if you will?

The GO light says, "Yes, it's time to reset my old, crappy beliefs" to gradually release from the old into the new and expanded realities. This example will give you clarity as I share a personal experience.

I tend to watch clients, friends, and family all at the same time share patterns that overlap, but it's like we're blind to our own patterns and rules. When I've been in a self-review mode, I typically make more of an effort to improve my physical health. I've been able to attribute my poor health to the same organ that's been addressed by multiple healers. My liver has been discussed by the MD, naturopath, Chinese medicine doctor, and energy healers – um, ok, ok, I finally got the message through my stubborn head. So, instead of giving my liver anything additional to process, my first thought was, let's lighten the load and detox it. The pattern of the root cause revealed my solution. Clear up the root cause. I had to acknowledge the same pattern everyone falls into: we avoid the root but treat the symptoms.

I discovered that I didn't only need to cleanse my liver, but I also had to clear out deep, old energetic clutter in every aspect of my life. At the same time, I came across an amazing liver flush. Just to clarify, it's not just a mind-blowing cleanse; it goes beyond physically clearing my liver. Detoxing the sludge in my liver also removed the emotional sludge attached to it, and I manifested this transformation.
(Book located on the EXPANSION Page)

How did I manifest this liver detoxing book to fall into my lap? I repeatedly asked my spirit guides to deliver true healing and vibrant energy every time I drank my

charged love water. I'm sure you're thinking…what's love water? I wrote "I LOVE YOU" on my water bottle, then I drank love all day long.
(Example on EXPANSION page).

In doing so, I developed a desire to detox more areas of my life that my soul was directing me to, in turn creating more energy overall. First, I felt a deep need to clean out my closet, which held old emotional memories. Then, after completing the liver flush, I was open to the release of emotional energy by letting go of all the years of liver stones which also held anger in my body.

Did I imagine drinking love water that said *"I love you, I love my vibrant energy and clear neutral mind"* would mean liver flush, cleaning my closet, and getting a *"Fuck the rules"* message in my mind daily regarding my career would be the outcome? No, I didn't plan any of it, but I disciplined myself daily to drink, read, and apply, even in tiny doses.

Does what we ask for look different from what we imagine? My example is proof. Almost always, what you want and what you get comes with an odd delivery when they appear. Does it make us more uncomfortable than we expect? Yes, because what appears is often against the guidelines we've been taught previously.

Let's get real. Check your rules… in marriage, health, wealth, money, societal status, intimacy, career, love, kids, and with yourself. What rules do you wish were different?
Whose rules are they: yours or someone else's?
Think about marriage.

- What if an affair is what could save your marriage?
- What if wealth is awaiting you only when you start a new career that fits your soul?

- What if trying to be what everyone else wants you to be means you're starving yourself to death?
- What if your own rules on how to live a great life are actually smothering your soul?

When will you wake the fuck up?

I'm frequently asked about astrology. "How much of this stuff about the planets is made up or real, Daune? Can we shape our fate based on the patterns of movement in the skies, or is our destiny already set?" My answer is that you all come in with an energetic tattoo of the galaxy the second you are born. But it's your free will that sets you on a path of high or low frequency.

Yes, your energy tattoo patterns are preset, but we must account for free will. You can change your energy blueprint as easily as taking a detour on a geographical map. You have free will to embrace, expand, or avoid your very clear patterns. It takes courage to open your warrior spirit. It takes courage to dig into the root of all things you value that we brush aside and for which we all make excuses.

Several clients have shared recently how their spouse, children, or friends have triggered them to remember old crappy thoughts they thought were gone. They're not gone until we check our rules of why we won't live our whole lives expanded. Are your relationships triggering you and causing you to think they're the reason you're miserable? They don't trigger us more; it's that we're not aware of our need to let go of playing small in scarcity, and your relationships reveal what you don't want to release. Those relationships are pushing your buttons. Your moon sign (check your free chart available on the EXPANSION page) is an easy way to reveal where your emotional weakness gets triggered by others…in both wanted and unwanted ways. Why are we afraid to go for more?

It's now time to start creating some expansion in your life, a.k.a. Taking your balls back (Extra support in *BALLS:* EXPANSION). Start living the life you came here to live instead of playing small roles set by someone else's rules carrying a scarcity mindset. Do you believe your soul, as brilliant and powerful as it is, doesn't know what rules can break you free?

EXERCISES

1. What's one thing you get triggered by easily? Body shame, financial awareness, career status, romantic relationships, spiritual values, emotional support, social pressure, communicating your truth? Write it down. (Use the EXPANSION PDF)

2. Write down one or two rules you've accepted but dislike. How does it make you lose power in the topics above? (Like going from 100 to 0 in a moment when it appears. Perhaps it scares the crap out of you?)

3. Write down one external source of distraction you use as a coping tool to avoid strengthening your weak spot from question one. Eating, drinking, TV binging, social media scanning, exercising, talking, shopping, and avoiding a conversation, to name a few.

4. Fuck those rules. Dig deeper to the root of those rules you feel give you social acceptance. Make your OWN F*ing rules. Write a rule you want changed. What does life look like without the rule you dislike in number two?

BADASSERY EXTRA CREDIT TIP

Take note of your coping tool and when you learned it to keep you in the safe zone. Does it still soothe you?

EXPANSION CHAPTER 3

Liver flush link page
ideserveitnow.com/tools

LOVE WATER
(see photo)

BALLS - Building Balanced Relationships
WINNING WHEEL
(see photos)

4

DRAMA STEW

...

"Every person, all events of your life are there because you have drawn them to you. What you choose to do with them is up to you." - *Richard Bach*

Drama is like an incurable case of loving the wrong person. Deep down, we want it to bring comfort and happiness to our lives. However, over time, it only hurts us. Over the years, the recipe gets lost in translation. For a long time, I struggled to understand the reason why we stay in the same place and do the same things while expecting different results. The answer is this: it's easier. We're comfortable when we do things the same way, even if it results in things we don't ultimately want. We fear change. Doing, watching, eating, etc., we have the power to keep our environment the same or change it. This is a very hard truth for us to accept. We have the power to avoid anything we dislike.

Just like a cook in the kitchen, we make a pot of stew called, "Days in Our Lives." This drama stew starts with a recipe. The recipe is one that we've come up with ourselves or that has been handed down to us through generations and is one that we've identified and followed. When drama shows up in our lives, it's hard to see that it's the result of our own doing. We choose to incorporate all the specific ingredients into our recipe. We put the people, the circumstances, and the material things (i.e., television and social media institutions, to name a few) we want in our lives and into our stew. They're our ingredients. But when the recipe we've chosen doesn't satisfy our cravings, we stir it, stir it, and stir it some more to see if we can get it to taste better, more to our liking. We stir it, hoping that it will improve. When we still get the same result, however, we don't feel any better.

Here's an example. I listened to a story from a client that sounded just like the story she'd told me before, more than once. Drama in her life. Over and over again, it was the same story but in different circumstances. I asked her what it was about that specific stew that sounded so delicious to her, but she didn't enjoy eating it. Her answer was always the same.

"I don't know. I don't like the ingredients or the people in it at all."
"Really? Well, you are the one who made it!"

She responded in denial, as we all do at first. "I didn't make it. Everyone else in the pot keeps messing up my life. It's not what I want. I tried to change it, but nothing ever works."

Remember, as hard as it is to hear this, we own the recipe for our drama stew. In other words, we're in charge of our lives. We are not victims! We choose to read, talk, and accept negative conversations, people, and negative energy in our lives. For example, my husband and I had overcome death and long-distance love, to name two biggies, only to have the state of Washington dictate "months of lockdown" for no reason, not based on facts but on fear. Do you think we accepted being told how to live our lives by others? Telling us what we could or couldn't do? Of course not! We found a way around it and kept living according to our truth that we would not negotiate.

I have a chapter in my book *Drama Detox* about swear words. "Can't" should be considered a swear word. (Link to full book in the EXPANSION) We ALL must stop saying it. I hope you can be inspired to embrace this philosophy we live by. We choose to focus on finding every solution that supports love for ourselves and our loved ones. We work around any roadblocks. It's time to eliminate "Can't" from our lives and take our power back. Otherwise, the external is in power. This is my wake-up call to you.

Do we tell others? Do we broadcast it? There is no need to force our stew and its ingredients on others. Do we get angry or disappointed sometimes? Absolutely, it happens, but it fuels our intention to live our lives on our terms. Could my husband and I have wallowed in a shitty pot of politician government drama stew? Absolutely. Instead, we found a way to live in a sovereign spirit, a state of courageous consciousness, affirming our power over ourselves. Nothing can block us from love. Love holds each of us accountable, and then we can hold each other accountable to that level. Are we holding ourselves accountable for the drama stew ingredients we each choose to cook as well?

Perhaps while reading this, you've had an epiphany and recognized the drama in your life. "How do I get out of this craziness?" Let's talk about Detox Stew.

The most important step in removing drama from our lives is awareness. So, congratulations! The fastest way to clean our own house is to become aware that it needs to be cleaned. Being aware of how often we use the word "can't" would be another great step. Often, we're just used to situations, so we miss the need to clean. This is called habituation when we become blind to an unhealthy situation or habit. What areas of your life could use a cleanse? Think about it. What areas could be labeled as having drama in them? Start to evaluate who is part of that drama. When does the drama happen? Where are you when it's happening? What's said to trigger it? Get the idea?

Can we see how we made a lifestyle from a recipe that we've been given for hundreds of years? Now, it's time for a new recipe. But how?

The next step is to ask ourselves what we want this recipe to taste like. Then, we need to learn about who we want to help us make this new recipe with healthy, vibrant, and delicious ingredients. A quick and simple way to start is to go online and search. When you get an answer you don't like, do the research and ask about it, ten times if you must, to make a recipe you do like.

TIP: Don't complain about the one television station, social media channel, medical doctor, or school that taught you one belief. Go back to the basics and ask yourself: If I cooked this stew (or experience) from scratch, what would I do to ensure I'm using the ingredients I love? Ask yourself, "Is it my truth?" Maybe, maybe not, but it's ultimately *your* recipe until you make a new delicious one.

EXERCISES

1. Write down one drama stew you've cooked for years or generations that needs a new recipe of love. (personal or professional experience) Is that truly your dream life? *(PDF Expansion to assist you: Circle the top 3 challenging areas of your life.)*

2. Identify and list the unwanted ingredients of the above-listed drama you experience in those areas of your life. (people, topics, feelings, etc.)

3. As the cook of this recipe, what small improvement could you make today in your drama topics?

BADASSERY EXTRA CREDIT TIP

Keep track of the times you say it throughout the day and see if you need a 'can't' reset.

EXPANSION CHAPTER 4
PDF Download
Winning Wheel

5

Pain Is Your Internal Healer

...

I teach this concept called clean sweep change. I'm sure you can guess what it means: one clean sweep. This is not the solution many want. They prefer to sugarcoat the truth instead of keeping it real with themselves. Our life experiences happening right now are no accident. They are the reality we're personally designing until we realize we can remove the parts we no longer want. Is light (truth) revealing our shadows (pain)? It's funny to me that we deeply desire the truth, yet it's the thing we fear to see most. I don't believe we fear the truth; we fear what the truth will ask us to decide. This or that?

When anger, avoidance, or anxiety appear, it's often previously avoided fears being revealed by Earth's new frequency of truth.

There's an old saying that goes, "The truth will set you free." But what does that really mean? And how can we be sure that we're living in our truth?

According to some, truth is simply spirit or consciousness, the truth of your soul living awake to its true purpose and sharing it for your highest good. So, in essence, awake and shining light with your truth is consciousness.

Others argue that the adage is outdated and that a new truth is emerging. They believe that we are evolving into a higher state of consciousness where we are more aware of our spiritual nature and interconnected with all of life.

So, which is it? The old truth or the new truth? Perhaps it doesn't matter. What matters most is that we're living in a way that is authentic to ourselves. When we do this, we open the possibility for real transformation in our lives and the world.

It's interesting to think about the different consciousness levels that exist on Earth. On the one hand, you have the old Earth, which is dense, dark, and survival based. Then, you have a new Earth, which is lighter, more connected, and thriving. It's almost like two different worlds existing side by side. The old world is slowly dying out while the new world is slowly emerging. And it all has to do with truth and consciousness. Those who are resistant to change often have a hard time seeing the truth because it contradicts their old reality. But if we can see past that, we will begin to adjust to a new reality where we thrive instead of just surviving. It may be disruptive and painful at first, but it's worth it in the end. We all have a choice about how we want to live our lives. What will you choose?

The new Earth we're now living on vibrates lighter, loving, tribal, and communal energy. So, if we're still hung up on an old reality (i.e. wanting our lives to return to "normal"), and it's pissing us off that it hasn't changed, understand we can't have our old lives back. Understand that whatever is pissing us off is a gift to wake us up. It can be painful in lots of different ways that are unique to us. This pain is meant to heal us.

The current energy of change is high and intense. It's forcing us to feel emotions we've avoided our entire lifetimes, perhaps even many past lifetimes. So, of course, we're going to feel irritated by crap with which we don't want to deal. That crap shows up as physical pain, emotional pain, or low spiritual faith, creating a dark and heavy feeling.

What happens when we turn the light on in a dark room? We see the unseen! Ah yes, the crap (our pain) we've kept hidden in the dark is revealed to be healed. The energetic light switch has been flipped for each of us, pushing us to upgrade all aspects of our lives. So, what does that mean? My easiest explanation is that there's intense light entering our cells to upgrade our bodies. It sounds scary if we can't see it. What's happening in our own bodies?

To keep this as simple as possible, the body is made of water, plasma, and electric currents. If any of those cells in our body are low, blocked, or turned off, we get used to compensating and functioning at that dragged-down speed. Now, imagine when they get stimulated and turned back online with full blasts of energy currents lighting up our cells. The energy will, in a sense, flip on the switch in our cells, which have adapted to functioning in a dark room, now causing those cells in our bodies to say, "WOW! I didn't even see this toxic debris in this room. Let's purge and detox this trash that doesn't belong here." That purge causes a reaction of release from our bodies' cells like a garbage truck dumping all the cities' trash at the dump. The body then feels the pull of heavy physical and emotional weight releasing! Sometimes this can be uncomfortable or even painful.

We must release old, dark emotions, memories, and beliefs that resonate at low frequencies of consciousness, like anger, fear, resentment, criticism, etc. This is what's happening to all of us right now, individually as well as collectively.

When our attention is pulled from divine universal truth and love, we focus outside of ourselves on other topics like food, TV, media, politics, sex, drugs, and substances, to name a few, so that we won't see the truth. We won't see *our* truths within if we're only looking outside of ourselves. We'll only see a diluted version that can be manipulated with our egos, thus losing sight of our true lighthouse state of bright love consciousness.

Any illusion of truth through another set of eyes demanding that we live in *their* truth and reject all loving truth within us is not higher consciousness of the divine. It's low consciousness that results in pain.

If we haven't done the work to release old, dark weight in our bodies, minds, and spirits, the intense light filling the Earth will feel like an intrusion or like a home invasion at night. If an intrusion occurs, it's one we've invited in. Our inner thoughts are asking for a lighter life, and we're unconsciously attracting the light to enter our reality.

Increased light blasts darkness up to the surface. Nothing will stay buried in the shadows as we move into a higher collective consciousness. The light reveals the internal body, mind, and deep emotions locked up, which now manifest as physical symptoms to get each of us to pause and address our inner shadows. It's like our souls are being upgraded with unexpected side effects from the upgrade. If you've avoided touchy topics in your life, you're likely to feel old crap surfacing for removal. What does this mean? Physical death? No, it's more of an emotional and mental death!

What you're avoiding is what you're feeling. I call these Pain Pillars (In Expansion)
- Abandonment
- Trust
- Security
- Shame
- Guilt
- Fear

The light appears outside of us to get us to see what emotions need to go to the dump. In other words, what's being lit up for us in the external world (what's upsetting us) is a hot spot of pain for us to heal within.

This hot spot is meant for us to see where we lost our power and take it back. Truth: We are processing our pain to heal ourselves into our Badass Power.

Too many want to label things so they can avoid the undeniable truth. This isn't woo-woo spiritual shit. This is the Age of Aquarius, the age of truth, as well as the generation of Aquarius, mavericks who are very present and will push this planet's humanity to the next dimension of love and community existence. Aquarius carries the energy of humanitarianism, group connections, and quantum science. The downside of this shift is that Aquarius has intense high-low events. Sudden bursts in/sudden bursts out … crickets and chaos, as I like to refer to it. Since we're each in charge of our new realities, what will we choose: toxicity or the truth? Will you shut off from a higher reality or upgrade to thrive?

Try this mantra: Repeat… *"I allow light to shine on my old toxic pain as it surfaces. I am open to seeing what the light reveals. I need a detox, and I am ready to release now because I am a Badass Warrior."*

Not "I have no choice but to linger with others in delusion and ignore the TRUTH."

Yes, there's one universal truth. It's neutrality, and that's your new Earth and new reality. Allow the light in. It wants to show us the way out of the dark, both internally and externally. No matter what we try to ignore, the light is showering down. As a badass boss, it's time to release and renew your badass self. Remember, you're the only one who can reset your true warrior consciousness. It's time to let go of what's not working. So, go out there and be the badass you were born to be!

EXERCISES

1. Whatever upsets you is your teacher. What upsets you right now? What does it want you to learn about yourself?

2. What is something you see that keeps appearing in your life that makes you sad, fearful, or angry, but if it's true, it forces you to choose a new path? (Use Expansion for assistance)

BADASSERY EXTRA CREDIT TIP

Can you view others in pain as simply being illuminated for the arrival of a lighter life?

Expansion Chapter 5

Pain pillar pdf

6

Are You Answering The Yeti?

...

In a world where we are constantly bombarded with outside noise and distractions, it can be difficult to stay in touch with our own hearts. But what if we could learn to tune into our hearts' frequencies and use it as a guide for our lives? By becoming aware of our hearts' truths, we would be able to more easily identify when we are out of alignment with our values. We would also be better equipped to navigate the sometimes-challenging waters of the external world.

It's as simple as asking our hearts. Does this feel fulfilling or draining? I can enter a room and immediately feel who's full of dark clouds as well as who's full of joy. I can be in a store and walk past a stranger and feel their joy radiating off them, and I can feel the weight coming from the whiny, needy customer wasting the employee's time at the checkout counter. It's you, and only you determine the brightness or dimness of your life. Essentially, we must become bosses of our own lives, guided by our inner compass. So, what are you waiting for? It's time to start tuning into your heart today and become a truth warrior by owning what the truth is radiating out of us at all times.

When we awaken to the truth, we dislike dishonesty, manipulation, and control that get us to do things against our core values. We start to feel uncomfortable, even frustrated. Why? The frequency of our heart conflicts with external nonsense. It may have been something true for us all our lives, but it no longer "feels" right in our hearts.

Our higher selves or spirit won't direct our compasses in the wrong direction. Our hearts put us on paths only for our highest good. Even if it's a good, ole, painful lesson we need to learn for growth, it's still for our highest good. Like a person pushing you out of the way of a moving vehicle that is about to hit you and their push may cause you to get scratched and banged up from the fall. It was ultimately to save you, not harm you.

What things are changing that were aligned with our old, programmed truth but are no longer aligning with our hearts' inner truth?

Anything not aligning that can push our buttons include Things, Thoughts, Truth, or all of the above.

THINGS: *(any 'thing' you can touch)* Two big ones below:

Consumption: money, meds, munchies, you get it, things. But let's just focus on food. Certain foods and beverages no longer feel good in our bodies. We find alcohol no longer assimilates in our bodies. Perhaps we can't drink as much as we used to. For example,

I'm not a big drinker, but now I feel off after just an occasional glass of wine. Simple water may taste different or be full of chemicals in varied places, and we notice. We are more aware. Maybe a greasy burger used to hit the spot, but now grilled, fresh, organic beef on homemade sourdough with a side salad makes you salivate.

Work: We're not feeling it at work like we used to. We question what else we could be when we grow up! I posted on my Instagram once about dropping off my youngest at college and realized I was being shown a vision of my reality, asking, "What do I want to be when I grow up?" Not only was she on an adventure to figure out her future, but so was I, if I was being honest, about how I wanted to truly live my life, like proving how it is possible to empower more while working less. I am intent on creating things with the highest vibration to match my thoughts and truth.

THOUGHTS: *(you have the power to change your 'thoughts' at any time)*

Friends & Family: Some relationships may split in ways we didn't expect. Furthermore, if they didn't have the label of spouse, dad, mom, sibling, aunt, uncle, or BFF, you wouldn't be friends. So, it's separating you from what no longer vibrates with love in your heart. Forever? Maybe not, but for now, it's the cause and effect of the lightening-up work you have been doing on yourself to feel lighter in your heart. If relationships in your life ignore the expansion you're striving for, they may be holding you back from growing. Your empowered thoughts must align with your truth and lifestyle.

TRUTHS: *(your spirit is your god consciousness, your truth GPS in a sense)*

Spiritual Beliefs: Our faith also isn't working the same way it did in the past. God, or source, is **not** in a box or a building; it's in our hearts. As we reach for others with similar spiritual beliefs, those who worshiped in the box with you may no longer align with your higher love frequency. This is often due to being taught to accept suffering and unworthy boxed programs. Source consciousness is love and acceptance, not self-sacrificing and suffering. Many religions still enforce this concept of suffering and sacrifice, and it isn't in alignment with the higher frequencies of love to which we're all awakening.

The story I repeatedly hear: *I do so much inner work and have been raising my frequency to be aligned with my truth, but I don't feel like it's working. Nothing is changing.*

I call this the yeti time. When you hear yourself saying, "I've been working on this a long time, and it's not working." I say add… NOT YET.

Recently, though, many have been calling me and saying it's happening, and I reply, It's YET time. "Yet," has arrived. I call it YETI time. You all know the sasquatch in the woods is not real, but many have said it is. The scary, big thing that's a myth? That's the YETI. It's big, powerful, and elusive as to when you'll see it, but you have faith that when you do, it's Yeti time!

It's time to start asking yourself, does "it" (*people, consumption, beliefs, environments*) things, thoughts, and truth hurt me or help me?
Is it *my* truth or *their* truth?

I prepare my private coaching clients for the awakening after-effects that will shift them following our sessions together. Your circle of influence will alter, because you won't feel comfortable vibrating at the old, heavy frequency that doesn't align with your new higher soul frequency. Are they bad or less? Not at all, it's just heavier than you prefer after unpacking your hefty drama bags.

So, the big question is, what is your soul calling you to do?
Are you willing to answer the call of your soul's truth?

This is scary because this is faith - faith in yourself, and the frequency of your soul. It's not a conditioned program. Faith dismisses your ego and doesn't care if you're accepted externally. Faith wants you to live expansively, engaged, and enlightened.

Many are not very happy in this life, I mean truly happy, not because they don't want it, but because they are unsure how to achieve it. Sadly, we're confused about how to expect happiness all the time. Sidetracking inner peace isn't an option any longer.

Your path is divinely guided. You are being called to answer the call of your soul's truth. It might be scary, and it might not make sense. But if you trust your soul's desires, you will live a life beyond what your programmed mind could imagine. Answering your soul's call is not a one-time occurrence; it's a lifelong dance. Deep down, you already know what you long for and what your soul yearns for. Whatever you are drawn to do is your truth.

Don't overthink it. Don't wait for permission. Just say yes.

Most people are waiting for a step-by-step plan before they make the first move. But intuition doesn't work like that. Your soul's blueprint astrologically doesn't work like that. It takes faith and courage to answer the call of our souls, and that's why most people don't do it. But you are not like most people.

You are in exactly the right place to answer that calling. You don't need to know the whole plan. You don't even need to know where it's leading. You just need to take the next step. No one has ever known the complete, perfect plan in advance. There is no right or wrong way to do it. We don't need permission from anyone else, especially the TV wizards who've become something out of the movie, "The Wizard of Oz." That film with the hidden little man "wizard" behind the curtain had more brains than the current TV wizards. Sometimes, the more resistance we have around answering our soul's call, the more important it is to our soul's growth to complete it.

When you trust this, you won't question the discomfort you feel from people, places, or experiences popping up from your past to help you correct your GPS direction.

EXERCISES

1. Are you answering your soul's call?

2. Evaluate past experiences revisiting you to evaluate what your soul deserves. Do they hurt or help?

BADASSERY EXTRA CREDIT TIP

What dream do you often imagine, hoping it's real, but seems like an illusion, like the YETI?

7

Awakening is a Choice, Not an Event

...

What is all this awakening mumbo jumbo anyway? What does awakening actually mean? Is it physically being awake or asleep, or is it some spiritually enlightened thing? Well, funny, it's a little of both. However, it's not an out-there thing; it's an inside job. One day, you realize the outside world isn't working for you, and you're miserable. You then start cleaning your house, so to speak, so you can live lighter, and ta-da! You see your world differently; you're awake.

The earth is experiencing a facelift. It's taking on a new, lighter look, and it holds new images we never thought possible. How did we get to this burning-down planet? Thousands of years of unhealthy voices have repeatedly told us that we have no power and that we're slaves to a corrupt system. Those voices have repeatedly reminded us how we'll always be separated from others who are better than us.

The thing that is so fascinating about this historical time on Earth is why so many are not asking, "Why the fuck would we do that?" By "that" I mean anything that doesn't lift us. We have blindly accepted what strangers have told us to do with everything in our lives. This has never made sense to me, not even when I was a child. I always wondered when I saw basic issues being distorted into more complicated issues, "Why do they make it so complicated?"

As I grew up, I was called weird and bullied by those who not only wanted easy, thoughtless answers but just accepted what they were told.

Yet, every boxed institution I attended ignited the same question inside me. Why the fuck are you making this so complicated? Why the fuck would I do that when it's stupid and the long-way approach? Yet, I just played along to get along. But inside, I knew better. Overcomplication felt like a whole scam, and total BS. Primary school and college programmed our learning with repetition and memorization over interaction that simply dumbed down society: medicine failed to heal people for good; religion deemed people bad from the get-go; the news was never nice; and television only showed depressing, unhappy outcomes; marriage was doomed from the start because people were in love with marketing fairytales and not each other. Children were ignored instead of loved, and natural healing was condemned as quackery. This is just scratching the surface. And you still wonder how we got here? For thousands of years, society has accepted an idiotic BS string of beliefs.

This is why I've been repeating the same "take back your power" and "deep dive for the truth" messages for the last 15 years. I've sought to reprogram our unhealthy patterns with a healthy dose of "Fuck no!!! I'm in charge of me!"

If nothing I teach is about the past, then why do I bring up all the boxes of the past? To remind each of you what's happened in your lives and why every box of illusion from the past no longer matters. What matters is fixing our perspectives now to get actual results that heal the very things we have been told are incurable.

It's time to stop seeing the illusions we are pushed to see and realize nothing from the pre-programmed past is in our favor. It's now up to each of us to decide to wake up. Everything in our realities that we dislike is on us to change within each of us first.

If you've focused on anything from the past you want to prove right or wrong, you are still sleeping. If you're focused on growing into the lighthouse you want to be now, then you're awake. You're awake when you're willing to flip the light on to see all that was hidden from you. You won't settle for a lack mentality another day.

Awakening is a choice, not an event. So many are awaiting an event or a storm! When you choose to live freely and to create the life you desire, you're no longer on an old, controlled Earth, and that, my friends, is when life gets so juicy and delicious. This is living in truth. Not to fear it but to learn to grow into your most badass self. There is only one truth! We decide to manipulate, avoid, control, or accept it.

Do you want the truth? What would you do with the truth if it shifted you out of your dark comfort zone? What beliefs are you so attached to that you refuse to see the truth? Yes, the truth can be subjective to everyone's perspective. So, just for a better visual, let's replace the truth with "reality."

Awakening is not a spiritual woo-woo experience most want to brush off. It's a choice to wake up and see any darkness that can be transmuted by simply being the light within yourself. That choice requires you to do inner work instead of a scaredy cat running away when you see what was in your dirty closet (or darkness). You may have a few shadows to address, but it's what the awakened person focuses on - being a bright lighthouse, not dark, judgy, and angry. This means being awake to your body, mind, and spirit. What do you need to see about your own life that you need to own? Which of these boxes (educational, medical, financial, marital, familial, etc.) affect you the most? What topic did you incarnate on this planet at the most historical time ever to shine light on?

You have a choice: to see your truth each day or accept strangers telling you their truth. What will you choose: to flip on the light switch or not? Will you open your eyes to the truth or stay in the dark?

Staying in the dark is old school, and the awakened world will expect you to upgrade your frequency to love and light. Badasses aren't getting lost in the lousy language. They live it daily by choosing to separate from whiners and choosing Love, Light, and Truth.

EXERCISES

1. What box (institution) in your life gives you the most challenges?

2. What areas are you willing to deep dive into and ask yourself why you accept this old, small nonsense mentality?

3. What truth are you willing to wake up to that you are avoiding but would set you free to live your best life?

BADASSERY EXTRA CREDIT TIP

Do you allow the whiners in your life to hold you back? Will you choose to tell them:
"I believe in you!" then simply move along and focus on you?

8

LOW VIBE EMOTIONS

...

Having devoted the majority of my youth to athletics and earning a college degree in kinesiology and physiology to master the intricacies of the physical body, I was intensely driven to satisfy my desire for physical and mental well-being. My insatiable need to grow strong, fit, and healthy, both physically and emotionally, persisted for years until I finally had an epiphany. No matter what I did with supplements and exercise, I was still miserable. I was still cycling with some sort of sickness. I was still anxious, and I was still not happy with my body. I asked myself why I wasn't better when, by society's standards, I was supposed to be improving. I looked fit and healthy, but I felt miserable.

So, by my standards, I was not feeling it. I was tired, sad, in pain, and being told to keep doing what I was doing. Well, that sounded like a bunch of BS being spouted off by medical doctors, therapists, and teachers whom I could see were miserable in their own lives.

I kid you not; one MD started crying about her cheating husband while I was on the table to seek her help for my own anxiety. Following her breakdown on my paid visit to her office, she prescribed me Valium. Yes, she gave me a pill to numb myself. An avoidance pill that I never took. I wanted to feel good, not numb with despair. Yes, that was a huge, "Wake-up, Daune!" moment.

Why did I look for solutions from those who weren't delivering the results I wanted? They didn't have solutions; they had band-aids. And I was not interested in band-aids. I was interested in tapping into my DNA and finding its switch to turn on my immunity and create all the things I was told were impossible or not normal.

Let me be clear. There is nothing normal or acceptable about feeling miserable, ever. Do not ever accept that answer from anyone. It's simply a cop-out answer because those "professionals" don't have a solution, and their egos are too big to admit it. Are there some exceptional MDs on the planet? Absolutely, I'm friends with a few. But the majority are simply caught in a system that has jailed them in a sense of band-aid relief.

In my search to feel better, what I realized is that mastering your body won't do shit if you're ignoring your low-vibe emotions and beliefs. We are spiritual beings having a physical experience. If we can open our minds to understand that we are simply energy plasma particles inside a skin suit, we can then start to see if we house low-frequency energy in our bodies. It's simply holding emotions of sadness, uncertainty, shame, fear, guilt, and trust blocks (expansion page). Our physical vessel has clogged pipes similar to our clogged sinks. Once we address the emotions clogging (or stopping) your cells from detoxing emotional buildup, you can see the pipes free up and begin to flow with high-vibe energy and feelings that bring you wholeness, happiness, and health.

We have been going about this whole thing all wrong. We have been addressing the symptoms and not the root, which is the clogged emotions. When I reference emotions, I don't mean falling into a blubbery mess of tears all day long. Although crying is very cathartic, it's not the basis of your health. Finding the root of the vibe energy you've been holding onto for so long is the first step of giving the body permission to begin functioning and thriving again.

So, where do we begin to access our trapped, locked-up emotions? I have created the R&R tool to help you clear emotions you may not even know existed. Does it matter when or where you acquired them? Not really. It's more about your readiness to be free of them.

The R&R tool (Located on the EXPANSION page) helps us tap into the three portholes of our energy grid. This tool assists in allowing the body to release what no longer gives your cells the protection they once felt they needed. The body will then do the work to release and renew on its own. But raising our emotional frequency starts with releasing low-vibe blocks and releasing low-vibe beliefs and words you use daily. When you refer to "my anxiety," "my disease," or "my fat," you embody and become the pain, so it will embed into all your cells, assisting them to become weaker at a wounded frequency.

The two tips to free the emotional low vibe frequencies are to verbally release them with the R&R tool and reconsider your verbal expression to others as "I am whole and healed," even if you don't feel it yet. Your cells will hear your words tapping vibrations of higher frequency intentions of wholeness. By simply speaking it out loud daily, saying ok, it's time to purge this old, low vibe crap. If it doesn't match my new frequency of love and wholeness, it is out. Your body will then attract the physical support, supplements, solutions, and activity that sets it up for the expansion and thriving you truly seek. The important part is once you attract a solution, you will need to act with your free will to see the new healer, take the new supplement, start the physical/emotional detox, or move your body daily to rewire your nervous system and vessel to a new frequency. Just by going outside daily barefooted and grounding your energy is the simplest free healing tool you can start while you read R&R to yourself. But it's always on you to take action. The solutions will arrive with your energy work, but action is how you align your body to your new mind and truth beliefs.

EXERCISES

1. Write down two low-vibe pain points you catch yourself speaking often. What words do you use such as *(I am fat, I am depressed, my disease, I don't trust…etc.)*

2. Identify the unwanted physical pain by which you feel repeatedly defeated. Close your eyes and ask, what does the pain want to tell you about its vibe? Write whatever comes to your thoughts.

3. Now, use the unwanted pain above and repeat your R&R daily until you begin to feel the shift in your health. You will attract synchronicity that brings you solutions you never expected.

BADASSERY EXTRA CREDIT TIP

Write on your bathroom mirror:

"I am whole and healthy. I love my body."

(use dry erase marker ONLY)

Expansion Chapter 8

Print And Read R&R Daily

9

Licking The Curb For Love

...

You have the marriage, dating, and the love you want.

You create your life based on your level of self-worth and self-love. Self-worth is rooted in truly knowing yourself. Knowing yourself means knowing your strengths as well as your weaknesses and confidently owning them. Confidently owning who you are without feeling a need to tiptoe around others' feelings or be someone you aren't just to be accepted. You will attract the love you deserve and some you don't deserve. It's time to heal your love wounds.

Yet, we rarely do the inner work to make our walk and talk match at all times. Instead, most people attract relationships or experiences to keep them safe and protected from seeing their low self-worth by attracting others with low self-esteem and then finger-pointing to deflect it away. Because your subconscious is unseen, it's hard to believe you would attract someone to trigger some sort of feeling inside - any feeling, for that matter, and often it's crappy feelings to just feel wanted ... even if those feelings remind you of the unhealthy love you witnessed as a child. In essence, we seek love to match how we know to be loved. Healthy or unhealthy? It was the love we learned, and we want it badly.

As hard as this is to wrap your head around, you attract your version of love. You attract your expectations of what you learned growing up. You are like a magnet pulling toward you those people with the same energy as you. The hard part is you are often attracting unhealthy love magnets. Most of us don't like to admit we attract unacceptable experiences we label as love. We attract abandoning, ignoring, manipulating, controlling, critical, dishonest, irresponsible, and more experiences that we confuse with love and then sugarcoat as acceptable. We all know this is not acceptable behavior and has nothing to do with love.

This is the greatest epiphany you can have. Like, wow, is that what I think I'm worth? Fuck NO!

We often find ourselves forming relationships based on unhealthy love lessons, influenced by distorted feminine energy and examples from our parents or those who shaped our early years. If the guidance we received during that crucial time wasn't ideal or, in some cases, was downright traumatic, it's important to acknowledge that while they should have known better, they gave us all they knew. I'm not excusing bad behavior here, but in the context of Mastering Badassery and truth training, this is about who you strive to become.

You're here to be your stubborn, rule-breaking self, not here to dwell in the past or play the blame game with adults who often had very limited tools to navigate differently. Also, there's that time, place, and picking your specific parents, and your personal blueprint tattoo. As we discussed already, you chose this life so you could break the unhealthy cycles and badass up.

It's time to take responsibility for any unhealthy love learned that you may be repeating now. You repeat what your ego determines is safe, which says that the old, unhealthy version is the love you should seek.

If you were to go out on a limb and do the opposite of that unhealthy version and love unconditionally, honestly, and transparently, your ego would trigger you to believe you are somehow looking for danger. Being your naturally loving self gets you in trouble, just as you learned as a child. You adapted and developed coping tools to stay safe, and now you bring them to every date and argument with your spouse and kids. This is where ownership comes in.

To simplify, you receive the unhealthy love you learned, period. Stop overcomplicating it with excuses such as: "Oh, I had great parents. They were perfect" or "My parents didn't raise me, so I don't have that issue with my grandparents (or others) who raised me." You chose those adults as a soul before you were born to raise you so you could wake up to your own BS and bust out. Now, many would say I didn't choose those parents. But we came in with specific missions for our earth journey, and we need a "support staff" in a sense to keep us on path, sort of like some etheric and

some actual real people angels. So, planning them to assist us with a little or a lot of pressure to learn is what we plan before incarnating on earth.
This is where life is not happening to you; it's happening *for* you.

My version: *"Life is not happening to you; it's being created by you, to match you, to awaken you."* So, refusing to look at yourself is essentially on you. All the stories, such as my marriage sucks, my husband ignores me, my wife nags me, my dates ghost me, my girlfriends are needy, my kids are animals, I get no respect from people…these are all nonsense.

It's time to own it. You attract what your energy pings out. If you refuse to look at the relationships that keep appearing in your environment, you are refusing to look at yourself and what needs to be addressed.

For example, marriage:
My spouse cheated, my spouse won't communicate with me, my spouse doesn't respect me, my wife keeps mothering me, or my husband is a workaholic.

Ok, now replace this list with I'm cheating on my own needs, I'm not speaking my truth, I don't respect myself, I refuse to nurture myself, I'm avoiding what brings me joy, I'm catering to them as an excuse to avoid working on me, I blame them for not taking care of me so I can get attention I am afraid to simply ask for, etc.... The list is endless, but you know what you blame your partner for; your own BS insecurities.

DATING:
They are flaky, they ghost me, they are dating more than one person, they won't commit, they don't want to meet in person, they are dishonest.

REPLACE THE LIST: I am being flaky, I'm not showing up as transparent, I'm afraid of a commitment, I'm afraid to be seen, I'm not being honest, I don't feel I deserve to be loved.

LOVE:
They are such assholes, they are ungrateful, they are manipulators, they are needy, they are always acting out.
REPLACE WITH: I am an asshole, I am ungrateful, I am manipulating, I am needy, I am insecure about asking for attention.

If you are afraid of someone seeing your flaws, you will attract people who don't see you at all. You can spin your reasons why you attract challenging situations in your relationships, but it's pretty simple. How deeply can you own your life? How badly do you want it? My husband and I have a phrase we use called *Lick the Curb.* We typically use it for health, but it applies to all aspects of our lives.

Basically, what it means is this simple question: Are you willing to do anything and everything to fix this situation? When my husband was very sick with cancer and we would experience a treatment setback, I would ask, where are you on a scale of wanting to try another option? He would say, "I'm willing to lick the curb if you tell me it will work." This is what we did by using a naturopath doctor, acupuncture, Chinese medicine, ozone, IV, meditation, detox, 30-40 supplements daily, fasting, zero sugar diet, deep rest, and even a small amount of chemo he did not want, but he was still willing to lick the curb at the end, and this is just the shortlist.

Again, this phrase applies to health, wealth, and love. You may be experiencing a rough patch in your life, but you have the choice to give up or to "lick the curb." It becomes a choice to accept one option and be let down, or it's a choice to do everything and anything possible to change your reality.

In love, my husband and I had a rough start in our marriage with life-altering challenges that hit long and hard. The one thing we didn't give up was asking: What do we want? Answer: A connected, free, and honest partnership. There were times we weren't feeling all three. But we would then regroup and find a way to reinstate what we expected in our marriage. We would ask ourselves and each other: *Are you willing to lick the curb?* In other words, what will it take to get us where we want to be? Each of us must own our own BS we bring to our relationships. Are we appearing as Awesome or Asshole? Here are a few examples.

LICK THE CURB DATING SUGGESTIONS

This is who I am and what I want, and I will not negotiate. I will make a talking point list to discuss with others. My bio will be pure and clear with my intentions. I will be honest, even if they are not. I speak the truth from the first text exchanged. I shine with the intention of what I truly want. I will make lists of questions or ways to express myself, if I am weak in how I express myself or struggle to communicate. I will not accept only one way to meet and connect with others. I will deep dive into body, mind, and spirit to send out (sonar ping) my desire for a life partner. I will ask my spirit guides to help me send out loving, connected, and committed life partner sonar.

LICK THE CURB MARRIAGE

This is who I used to be, honey, but this is who I choose to be now. I will not negotiate my core values. I will fill them in myself, and I would like you to join me. I will attend necessary courses, read these books, and fill myself with the love I desire. I'd appreciate it if you'd join me. I believe in you and know you will when you are ready.

You must be the change you want to see, not the critical, judgy rule-maker who says, "You need to fix me; I have zero responsibility and act like a victim when I don't get what I want" (who simply resembles a wounded, unhealthy love partner acting like a 5-year-old). If they aren't meant to be part of your growth journey, this is how you know. But not until you know the real you and can share it with confidence.

LICK THE CURB LOVE SUGGESTION

I choose to reprogram my actual cellular DNA daily with healthy love for my body, mind, and spirit. This includes lovingly filling my body with TLC and rest. Putting loving and inspirational words into my mind daily about new things gives me confidence. I talk daily to spirit about how much I love every cell in my body and my life. Praying and using mantras for solutions to bring in healthy love daily. Then, I have the courage to do what is likely the opposite for me if I learned unhealthy love. When licking the curb of love, I am willing to fight for growth no matter what it takes.

Remember: you are a warrior, and badasses are stubborn rule breakers, so break the white picket fence rules and rise to healthy love.

Your DNA is fried because it's been living against its natural state of love. It's been living in a state of survival and suffering. Courage is required to fight for what you want. Sometimes, my friends, you may be alone until you realize that you are beautiful, loving, and kind. You must be willing to release and reset what no longer serves you by owning your own BS. This is not easy because most want to be rescued.
However, we are in warrior mode, not rescue mode.

When you attract crappy dates, have arguments with your spouse, or have conflicts with your kids, it's your opportunity to decide how badly you want healthy love with each person. Are you willing to lick the curb? Do you actually want healthy love, or do you want the idea of it? All of your excuses, all of your reasons for not living the life you want, are on you. All of the greatest parts of you are up to you. It's not technology's fault, your history, your bad luck, or your bad genes. It's you deciding to rewire your reality. What do you want?

Now, do whatever it takes!

EXERCISES

1. Are you ready to lick the love curb?

    How badly do you want it? REALLY badly, or do you think that great love, health, and wealth would just be a nice idea?

2. On a scale of 1-10, what are you willing to do to get it? Rate Yourself:

    10 (Really Badly) - 5 (It's new to me, but yes) - 1(Not interested in Badassery)

3. Make a list of every possible thing to improve it. What is every possible way to fix love or whatever the challenge? In and out of the box.

BADASSERY EXTRA CREDIT TIP

Write a list of the other areas of your life where licking the curb would change it.

Expansion Chapter 9

Shower Talk- Talk to your physical or emotional pain.

10

Neutral Isn't Nice - It's Nothing

...

Change in our lives is here, and it is happening now. We are finally in a state of renegotiating our soul contracts for why we came to Earth. This process requires quiet time and discernment. A time with no external stimulation influencing your mind, so your soul can speak the truth. It's time to just be, instead of feeling pressured to become what the external tells you is good for you ... some external realities that which you will never speak to or meet. Polarization at its best. The masters are those who can stay in neutrality and become an unmovable lighthouse. Lighthouses are neutral; they don't have an opinion of what boats can or cannot use their guiding light. They just shine.

Neutral is "I CAN," and I am preparing you to be open-minded in this chapter. Divisiveness isn't neutral; it is living in a state of polarity that IS slowly dissolving. As each day, month, and year ticks by, all political sides, religion versus spirituality, big pharma versus naturopathic medicine, physical versus energy, and education versus quantum downloading are all undergoing massive transformations. It's all a pendulum that will swing less and less until it settles into the center as truth. I get it. It's hard to shine when our lights are pounded daily with "can't."

Do you accept "can't"? Did you learn "can't" as your truth? It's not true; it's total BS. Yes, YOU CAN. You can heal anything, but first, we each have unfinished business personally, professionally, or emotionally to journey through to get to a neutral, calm state. Why don't we just choose calm? It's pretty simple: we won't be able to take an old scarcity mindset with us into the future. Still, we have some remnants which linger. It's futile to avoid seeing the dark anymore. When it appears, it's up to us to *see* the experiences we may have supported for years, perhaps even our entire lifetimes, and then one day, we must trust we're ready to release this belief in exchange for peace.

How's this shift appearing? Again, it's simpler than we often realize. Anytime we hear "can't," a shift is triggered. To be clear, I do not enjoy it when shifts trigger me either. I have felt my own physical and emotional energy affected when I release old memories and see new realities. I had for quite a long time experienced waking up at four a.m., or other odd times, irregular sleep patterns, strange dreams, random old emotions appeared, and played small in old patterns reappearing that I needed to detox for good. Was any of that fun or welcome? Not really. But it all appears to assist us. Even as prepared to upgrade my reality as I was, it still rattled me until I embraced the truth. I manifested this shit so I would stop accepting crappy experiences that required me to pull weeds from my garden.

Let's say, for example, I would wake up at 3:14 in the morning. Instead of getting upset that I was up, I would choose to release the old, frantic, worried pattern by saying, "Okay. I guess I'm up. I'll sleep when I'm tired later." We're releasing old energy inside ourselves. It's like oil and water. We're water, and anything unwanted in our lives is oil. From now on, instead of living in a state of fear, ask, "Why am I suffering?" or "Who's causing me to suffer?" Start opening your mind to: "What would a master do?"

Knowledge does us no good if we're unwilling to change, if we aren't willing to begin seeing our own lives through neutral expansion lenses. Anything appearing as external control is the universe twiddling its thumbs, waiting for us to turn it into a "can" instead of a "can't." We are the change! If we can see our expanded selves, we must be open to being squeezed dry of our old selves.

What does that mean right now? To squeeze anything requires pressure, so it's time to make peace with the pressure you manifest when you imagine an expanded life for yourself. What does squeezing old crappy beliefs and emotions out of you feel like?

Old-self energy purging appears in the form of pain, headaches, lightheadedness, anxiety, sadness, exhaustion, confusion, job loss, money strain, challenging children, sassy spouse, or loneliness and then once you acknowledge the feeling you dislike, it may shift to clarity, weird cravings from salty to sweet, weight gain/weight loss, old triggers and addictions, or ear ringing, and more of any combination which appears not to hurt you, but to slow you down giving you time to observe your life to make a choice. "Oh wow! No thanks! I'm good. I'll exit that crappy scene I have been avoiding. I'm ready to grow into my badass spiritual power." Knowing who we want to be neutralizes the negative energy. We'll be less interested in holding on to anything that constricts us, weighs us down, or shackles us from all we want. Whether you have believed it for 40 years or not, addictions, anger, criticism, separation, and fear are all man-made to keep you feeling small and incompetent.

Source consciousness is a collective tribal experience. We all help each other by encouraging each other to be our most badass version of expansion. What helps with that? Imagine you are a wet rag being twisted and squeezed to release all the last unwanted drops of water you hold to speed up the drying time. Your body and soul squeeze out all negative energy that you have allowed to water down the truth, such as our last drops of fear, insecurities, and excuses for not growing. We aren't small. We're spiritual warriors who have come to live our highest truth. What is that truth? It's up to us to understand who we are, not who others tell us we are.

Three ways to stay neutral.
1. Learn about your North Node on your astrological birth charts, a.k.a. a blueprint of your purpose. (EXPANSION: Medicine Wheel Course to learn your personal North Node)
2. Ask ourselves: What am I good at, or what's easy for me?
3. Get tunnel vision on that topic to live your truth.

We each signed a contract to come here and be alive during this time of humanity's awakening to shine our brightest light. What that means is that we came to shine like a lighthouse for anyone "*lost at sea.*" We didn't come to belittle, criticize, or hurt anyone, or hurt ourselves. Lighthouses are immovable with everlasting brilliance. They don't give a shit if there's a raging storm around them or a sunny day. They just shine!! They're stable and unmoving. You can choose to be the lighthouse, or the boat lost in the dark sea.

- Will you have days that feel like setbacks? Yes.
- Will you have days you need to simply sleep it off? Yes.
- Will you have days you need to purge with tears of insecurities? Yes.
- Will you have days when our pain reappears, and you think we've made no progress? Yes.

These are simply recalibration days of our light's dimmer switch. We're still lighthouses, just a dimmer bulb that day.

Spiritual warriors don't ask anyone to become a lighthouse or to stop being who they are. They simply shine their natural gifts. What do I mean by gifts? What we're good at. Accountant, mechanic, chef, healer, mother, CEO, teacher, gardener, artist, writer, entertainer. The list is endless.

I'm on a mission to raise the self-worth of the planet and help you see your infinite potential by expanding your consciousness. Your gifts are needed by many; your suffering doesn't help anyone. From now on, when we're told no or being controlled, all we need to say is: "Yes, I can!" Do not negotiate. There's always a way. Remember the last chapter on *Licking the Curb?* I mean, there's ALWAYS another way.

The new earth is about expanding "I can" energy, not the sacrificing, small, "can't" energy. If we simply shine, we'll begin to heal, attract healing, and, most of all, find neutral. Neutral is where we are at peace. It's where there's no this-that, me-them, right-wrong; it's just truth. It's not good or bad; it's just the truth.

Some truths will trash old beliefs. Some truths might hurt. As long as they allow us to expand, it's the only truth that serves us. If that's not the case, then we're not in a neutral state; we're in old patterns, and that's super ok. But if you are working on expanding your light, you will find it increasingly difficult to listen to or even see the whining, complaining, and resisting-change boats out in the ocean. Some boats will remain unwilling to accept a lifeline or refuse to release old beliefs, behaviors, or brokenness.

Here's the truth: You don't have a choice. The future is love, and resisting seeing the areas where you need to change is what will keep you in the "I can't" version of prolonged pain.

I am often asked how these changes of energy affect me. "What happens in your truth lighthouse, Daune?" That's a valid question, given teaching truth is my life.

Even when you shine bright like a strobe light and shine your best self, you must find neutral. Often, like everyone else, I'm caught off guard when chaos appears until I see patterns (which I love). I didn't catch interactions like this until I picked up on a pattern I saw repeatedly. I'd go to a restaurant, or a store and be ignored by the clerk or wait staff who'd stare right at me. Or they'd miss my order, repeatedly forget parts of it, or give me the wrong items. It was like I was invisible, right in front of them. The rest of the table received their items, but it was like I wasn't there. I could have gotten angry, but I sensed it wasn't personal. So, how do you adapt? With neutral questions.

I asked one argumentative waitress once, "Are you upset with me?" It was as if I'd flipped a switch by nicely asking. She literally came back online, finally made eye contact, and replied, "Oh, no. I'm just blunt sometimes," and proceeded to lighten her tone and attention. Bottom line: it's not personal if *we* stay lit even when they aren't. Being bright doesn't necessarily make life easier; it just makes you more content and at peace. Such a place of neutrality allows us to see how the boats are still in the lull of the rhythm of their old habits and unaware that they can choose to snap out of it.

That's what our lights do. Each time we shine, we snap someone awake. Say nothing, share nothing, just shine…and be our best, badass, talented selves. The higher we grow and the lighter we become, the more connected, not separated, we are with others. Those who grow with us are equal in light. So, there's no division, polarity, or separation between me and them. No hate or criticism, only allowing them to choose their journey.

If a dark memory surfaces, don't go backward. Stay lit, knowing the old oil will burn off. "I can" is a clear intention. Let's manifest our greatest dreams. There's a dark energy push from the TV wizards. Let me be clear. Anything digital is the wizard behind the curtain controlling what we see to make us believe what they want us to see, not what is necessarily the truth. They rarely, if ever, offer solutions, only suffering. For fifty-plus years, this has been happening, so it's not a new revelation.

It fascinates me how so few people question why, for hundreds of years, we have been, and still are, told there is no cure, no food, no safety, and no security on items that have multiple alternatives. Why are we not using our warrior skills to find an alternative? Why do we still accept old beliefs that stop us from finding healthy, organic, natural milk to feed babies? Why aren't we looking for organic protein powder to feed ourselves if the shelves are empty? Why is it not our first instinct to find an alternative natural remedy instead of a pharmaceutical remedy?

We aren't helpless, yet we're told we're victims of scarcity and shortages. We're not being reminded to use our powers to find solutions. This is TV wizard bullshit when they never offer solutions to what we can have. Instead, they hammer home what we can't. The surplus of alternatives is remarkable! Time to turn up our lights and make our fucking motto, "YES, I CAN!" If you don't like what the options are, it's time to find a truth that frees you. It's mind-blowing that we all have supercomputers in our hands, yet we accept being defeated so easily. For example, what if there's no baby food? How about feeding them real food? Every kitchen has a blender to make baby food without adding toxic preservatives. How do I know? I did it. I had a preemie baby sensitive to everything.

We've been in overdrive mode for so long that shifting to dream mode is foreign. Design it and trust divine delivery. We're ending our people-pleasing energy by shifting into truth. It's Zen peace. "Can't" is a swear word. Yes, you CAN, and, yes, you WILL, because you are spiritual warriors. Zen neutrality means forgoing your nice people pleasing with the light of truth and living your best life until those around you make their way to shore. It's not mean or nice. It's simply nothing but a neutral state. Just shining Light.

EXERCISES

1. When old dark memories that scare you pop up, write them out in detail and burn them. This is an old contract. Go to the sink and tear and burn that contract.

2. Write the feeling you would prefer to feel instead from this day forward on a new page and burn that as well.

3. What would a Master do? They would find a solution to their peace. Not accept suffering and scarcity.

4. What is your truth? What are you good at, or how is your North Node (birth blueprint expansion) calling you to shine your light?

BADASSERY EXTRA CREDIT TIP

When you are told no,
what will you do differently to make it yes for you?

Expansion Chapter 10

Zodiac Wheel is Your Medicine Wheel Course
Free Astrology Wheel for North Node description.
(symbolizing your life purpose)

11

SUGARCOATING AND ADVERSITY

...

What does life look like without sugarcoating? Would it surprise you that this topic is avoided the most in my coaching practice? It's all the things you wish to improve in your life, yet you ignore the discipline it takes to get them. We all try to ignore the root or block. Sugarcoating examples look like this:

- Ignoring a cheating spouse, yet you know something is off.
- Ignoring a belittling spouse, yet you know you deserve respect.
- Ignoring your weight or pain in your body, yet you know focusing on *you* solves it.

- Ignoring a wife who drinks too much and covering up for her in public, so you don't have to lose what you built together.
- Ignoring a child begging for attention through outbursts or failures, but you scold them instead of getting to know them.
- Ignoring the Debbie-downer in your friend group who depresses every social event, yet you put up with her just to not mess it up for future events.

The list is endless with examples. Do you get sugarcoating? Avoiding the hard choice doesn't make life easier and free to be you. Avoiding the root of what's causing these events is a good indication of why the experiences stay blocked. Because you aren't usually avoiding the experience blocking your success, you are avoiding the root that is often repeating from your childhood. It's avoiding TRUTH.

When I realized, I was born to raise the self-worth of the planet with personality mapping, I was excited and disappointed all at once. Sharing my gift was not an easy pill for others to swallow. The pill of TRUTH. Do I serve the sugar-coated pill or the nasty truth? The big hurdle is that many don't want to know the truth about themselves. This seemed so weird to me until I understood why they didn't want to know.

Understanding yourself creates responsibility. Understanding yourself is the red-hot coal many don't want to touch. If I don't know anything better than my sad/difficult/unfortunate reality, I don't have to own it because it's all I know. But if I do, I must take responsibility for a life of growth and ownership. This is your TRUTH, and the TRUTH scares people, not for what it represents but for what it will require of you to change.

For most of my career, many have asked why I use astrology. It's fast and easy for me. It's not different from any other personality mapping; it's how the personality map is used that counts. I don't believe any planet, person, or thing has any more or less power over us. I simply want to understand you and the galaxy blueprint with which you were born so I can appreciate the lessons you chose to learn. Our lessons are all different. But the one thing that holds true for every human on this planet is that there are no accidents, and every chart I see shows your beauty and talents. You are gifted and perfect just being you.

When you respect your character traits enough to understand how they affect everyone around you on many levels, you have the power to stay in a state of strength over being victimized. Learning your map determines your relationship reality, or how you get along with others. Your energy will have an impact on every room at all times.

So, avoiding any tools that interpret your character traits is simply neglecting your own physical, mental, and spiritual health. Any tool is a gift when you use it. The fantastic thing is that all the personality profile maps are the same. They just use different languages.

Perhaps this clarifies why understanding someone's blueprint is so vital when they are born with challenges and gifts, and, as you can guess, we all focus on the challenges the most. When I hear the phrase "Why me," I get it. I have been in the same place many times in my life. I asked the same question. Be honest. How often have you asked yourself when sorrow, debt, pain, sabotage, mean people, failure, and disappointments appear…WHY ME?

Let me be clear… We each 100% design our relationships and realities with our beliefs and energy. A version of you already exists to win, and it's at a

different vibration than the version of you who asks, "WHY ME." The winning version does not accept your weakened version. The winning version requires you to see life with a badass attitude. The challenge is that we believe what is out in the world is crap and that we just have to put up with it. WRONG!
Your current reality is a reflection of your relationships. When you choose the truth you want to express through kindness and compassion, there's no room for despair, depression, anxiety, or sadness. By releasing emotional shackles to how you feel the world <u>should</u> behave to make you happy, you grow disciplined and empowered to go after what you want. You have to decide on the life you deserve to live, or, even better, the relationships with which you deserve to surround you.

Repeat this phrase five times. Ready? Go:
I DESERVE IT…I DESERVE IT… I DESERVE IT… I DESERVE IT…I DESERVE IT.
Now, what are you thinking?

My intention for this book is to bring you to a lighter, easier understanding of the Universe and how you fit into this infinite Universe, not just this earthly planet. I want you to see how you fit into it, depending on whether you sugarcoat adversity in all relationships, or step into what you want. Sugarcoating, i.e., taking the easy way out and avoiding the truth, leads to self-sabotage in relationships. ALL of them.

I guarantee you, there isn't a person on the planet who hasn't encountered adversity.

Most think I'm kidding when I reference getting bigger balls, but I'm not. As I discuss in my book, *Balls - Building Balanced Relationships,* "Testosterone is referred to as the hormone of strength, and it's needed to grow muscle. You will continue to meet roadblocks if you are all yin or feminine softness." With the "I'm so kind and good to everyone" mindset, the "why me?" attitude, you have no balls by giving up your power.

Yet, I have not met one client who has the life they dream of deserving. Why????

Because when I hear, "Why ME?" I get to deliver the million-dollar answer. You are used to the old vibration of scarcity and adversity, and it's familiar. So, you have attracted your version of unhealthy love.

This is scary for us to admit, but you like it. You like knowing what to expect. Even if it's crappy and traumatic, you know how to navigate that type of storm. Happy sunshine is, in a sense, adverse to what you have been programmed to believe you deserve. In any relationship, it's easier to accept the limitations than to be expansive and deal with the aftermath of rocking a boat. Yet, neither of you is happy. When you step out of your comfort zone, of course, it is uncomfortable. Do it anyway. Do things you wouldn't normally do, because they will make you better.

Then, prepare for the "Well, I'm doing the work, but they are the problem" viewpoint that may arrive. Good luck selling that one to me. I have been coaching and training others for 30 years, and I am equally guilty as charged. When partners in my relationships were repeatedly unfaithful, I had to own it when my girlfriend asked me why I thought that was happening. I knew immediately. I'll give you one guess as to why I kept attracting unfaithful relationships.

If you said because I was not committed and that I was attracted to the easy way out (i.e., to blame them), BINGO, you're right!

Here's where it gets fun, and the adversity part kicks in. You need adversity to make the life you deserve. The bigger the dream, the more adversity you will need to prepare you to grow into who you need to be to live at that frequency. You will have to show persistence. If you don't, you will receive roadblocks to your dreams. When you resist those roadblocks, you've made it clear to the Universe that you are not ready for what you truly want. The Universe will send you things to see if your old patterns still shackle you.

Energetically, you will experience tests, in a sense, to see if you are becoming the person you are energetically sending out in your meditation, mantras, and prayers. You receive versions of yourself to see if you are in true alignment with your wish.

If you are not ready to step into TRUTH and you stay stuck, you are saying to the Universe, God, and Spirit, "Screw you, I'm not interested in being a higher vibration and getting the wish I just told you I wanted." The patient Universe says, "No problem. Screw you back. That is your vibration, and you will receive more of the old pattern until you step up and change your frequency." You cannot live in a new vibration with your old patterns and behavior. You must be open to the shift. Stop telling the Universe what you want, and then, when it presents adversity shifting your compass in a more desired direction, you tell it to screw off. Stay on the uncomfortable, expanded channel, even if it's not familiar for a while.

It doesn't have to feel good, but it must be non-negotiable for you to own the new frequency of your sonar. Submarines never send out a sonar ping they don't mean. Their signal is intentional. Most of us aren't aware that we are all sonar sending out vibrating energy. Let's look at what you vibrate out so you can see why you draw the relationships you do.

There is no need for pity parties, but there is a need for clarity and understanding. Validation is vindicating.

Let's be clear about the two reasons we sugarcoat our lives. Either we don't have tools, or we don't want to let go of what we know. We settled. Settling is an easy, comfortable state. It's what we know. We fear letting go of shitty. We've been programmed to believe shitty is better than ending up with nothing. Consider how nothing means neutral, however, which leaves a space for you to attract what you want instead.

The key is not to sugarcoat your life by thinking you are doing ok when, in reality, YOU AND ONLY YOU ARE neglecting your truth. When you are unhappy, it is 100% you accepting and repeating old, crappy behaviors.

What should you do? Ask yourself what one topic you are disappointed with in your life. Then wipe off the sugar and ask yourself what do you avoid taking responsibility.

EXERCISES

1. What relationships do you sugarcoat the truth, so you don't have to rock the boat?

2. In what area of your life do you continue to experience adversity?

3. Open Expansion page: WINNING WHEEL. What topic is your weak spot(s)?

4. FILL IT UP. What is one thing, if you did it daily to address the above-written weakness, would strengthen you forever?

BADASSERY EXTRA CREDIT TIP
If you stopped sugarcoating for others, what would change in your life?

EXPANSION CHAPTER 10

Use the Winning Wheel to determine where you are sugarcoating, and you should be winning instead.

12

ARE THE SIGNS REALLY EVERYWHERE?

...

Have you ever wondered if the Universe is trying to tell you something? If so, it could be coming through your dreams, repeating numbers, conversations with friends, meeting strangers, social media, license plates, songs on the radio, cloud shapes, or even animals crossing your path!

Are you feeling spiritually impoverished? You're not alone! I've found myself chatting about this topic with others multiple times. If we feel like our prayers or mantras aren't being heard, perhaps it is because the language of spirit isn't well understood by us humans. Spirituality has always come naturally to me. Since my early days, conversing with the divine through prayer, mantras, or even shouting for help has felt like second nature—a language we both understand.

It felt like I would receive an answer indirectly through energy symbols. This takes time to learn how your personal guides communicate with you. Animals, numbers, or people, but they are sending you guidance.

It might feel like a code at first, but understanding how energy works is key. Picture an animal showing up on your path - what does its symbolic meaning tell you? So, for example, when the roadrunner came to visit me in my yard for two weeks straight, I finally thought oh, this little guy may be bringing me a message to my current requests for help from my spirit guides. After a simple Google search on animal totem roadrunner meaning, the message was very clear, and I just shook my head and laughed. The meaning and message were more of a confirmation I was on the right path.

With research and practice comes clarity, and comprehending those messages from spirit becomes as easy as reading Morse Code! My skill of learning to talk to Spirit took some practice and research on what these recurring creatures had symbolized when they came along my chosen path. This is how I learned to understand and decode messages from above.

I started paying attention and started piecing together any clues. Soon enough, patterns began to appear. Think of these as direct messages from source or angels that are aimed at replicating your innermost thoughts. And, when a message comes in response to what's happening inside your head, change up your mental chatter vibes if they're not delivering the desired result! That's what Spirit gives you back, even if you don't want it. They match your energy vibe for vibe and thought for thought.

So, get clear regarding what you need help with, and then seek the Universe's guidance along the way. The signs are everywhere. Your ability to be present will determine how well you receive the appearing message.

My client shared with me in a session recently that she had a cracked foundation in her home. I immediately saw it as a sign from the universe alerting her. Interestingly, her house description was an exact match to the cracks in her emotional foundation. She felt unstable and insecure. That is a message from spirit expressing the need to clean up her internal foundation, and the rest would fix itself. It's really that simple, but you must be open to seeing how everything is connected. Even your home's foundation is a frequency match to the foundation of your thoughts.

Remember to embrace when you get a sign. It's in response to your mental chatter. If you don't like the message, change the chatter or be more specific on what you want the universe to help you with.

I often hear from clients that I want a new relationship. However, clarity is crucial. If, for example, your partner is a drug addict and you say you want a new relationship but don't address your own inner addiction to chaos, then another new alcoholic appears as a new relationship. This is what your request sounds like to the universe. But if you aren't clear on what kind of relationship you specifically want, or if you are not being the person you expect in return, i.e., a healthy and strong life partner, the universe will deliver a vague relationship. You keep attracting unstable people, because the messages you send out to the universe are unclear thinking and ambiguous actions. Source replies to you in living color. This applies to all requests like improving your marriage, finances, parenting, and health. It's all a reflection of your energy. So, ask for assistance from the universe through signs to guide you to healthier versions of the dream of health, wealth, love, and abundance you want.

EXERCISES

1. Write down a few signs you see repeating in your life.

2. How do these signs reflect your feelings about yourself? (For example, if it keeps appearing, Google animal totem "dragonfly" or angel number 444. Broken pipes in your home? Check yourself on what's leaking energy in your soul?)

3. What sign is asking you to make the biggest change to achieve your true dream instead?

4. Keep a journal or pictures of repeated signs and go back and see the patterns of messages, which are all similar and guide you.

BADASSERY EXTRA CREDIT TIP

Give spirit your own symbol to send when you need a "YES" message on things you're asking for guidance on. Pay attention when you see it.

13

INTENTIONALLY BURNING INTENTIONS

...

You hear about burning ceremonies on new moons and full moons all the time. So, what does it mean to burn your intentions?

Burning intentions is an ancient ritual that symbolically gives messages to the Universe. Science may not fully comprehend this, but something about writing down our goals and burning them creates a unique resonance between us and the Universe that allows us to believe we can make those dreams come true! Energy is energy; it cannot be destroyed. It can only be transformed into another form. So, taking energy from your soul and using the pen as a magic wand, in a sense, creates a wave of energy with your intended life plan and transforms your energy of thought into the energy of a thing.

But why wait for new moons or full moons? Take control now by utilizing this powerful practice weekly. Spend time focusing on what you desire with clarity, write it down, and then take a match to it. Trust with confidence that your wish will be granted.

Burning intentions may be symbolic to some, but it's simpler than that. It's like shouting to the Universe, "I don't need to keep reading this. I trust my intentions are my truth and are clear." If you truly believe the words you write to spirit, then to burn them is to release them with confidence and trust their return to you in a physical manifestation. Now, let's go through the steps.

1. Write your intentions on a piece of paper or sticky note.
2. Burn the pages in a bowl.
3. Release the message to the Universe and trust your intention will appear.

The intentions are not the most important part. It's about writing with clarity. It's about burning. It's trusting. It's the inner belief that attracts it to you.

As for what to write, all topics are fair game: love, communication, money, kids, career, and friends. Remember: clarity, burn, trust, and believe.

EXERCISES

1. Grab a stack of sticky notes and a heat-resistant bowl.

2. Write a few things you intend to create for your dream life. (Make them big! God and the universe don't play small, so you are also done playing small.)

3. Get a lighter and burn them in your bowl.

BADASSERY EXTRA CREDIT TIP

Do your next burning ceremony under the light of a full and new moon. Full moons are for closure, and new moons are for beginnings.

EXPANSION CHAPTER 13

Burning Intentions at Home:
Picture diagram included.

14

Truth Consciousness

...

How do we elevate our consciousness? By consciously choosing a frequency and committing to it. The only way we escape the chaos swirling around in our lives is by changing our frequency. The only way we can change our frequency is by changing our consciousness, and we change our consciousness through intentional living. Intentional living is choosing a path and giving it all your faith, will, and commitment to see it bloom. So, intentionally choosing to be willing, neutral, courageous, trusting, optimistic, understanding, forgiving, affirming, successful, loving, loveable, confident, free, etc. Simply choosing the life that resonates with you and committing to that life changes your frequency. Being conscious of your vision creates it in reality.

Here's an important tip to gain clarity on your visions. We can see and hear our dreams more distinctly when we are quiet. They can vibrate like sonar out to the universe more clearly as well. This is how we start to live our truth.

I have shared for years that we have been living through the lowest period of spiritual and emotional poverty in the history of our planet. Many have found this to be true through awakening. Awakenings have been arriving subtly with pokes and illogical situations you know are significant but didn't realize previously its power over you. Awakenings have also occurred more dramatically, as they have for the last several years, through the destruction and dismantling of old systems, such as institutions that only gave you one answer, option, or outcome as your only solution for success.

So many of us were led to believe the "Wizard of Oz" was simply a movie, only to find out the movie is a pretty accurate description of the reality in which we've all been living. However, as we awaken, we recognize that we are the main characters in our own film, and we can redirect this show called "Life" any way we like. We do not require a wizard to save us. We no longer need the "Wizards" from T.V., social media, the medical field, or anywhere else to tell us how to live our best lives. We know what our best lives are if we get quiet and listen to our hearts.

- Are you ready to stop waiting for someone to tell you what you want?
- Are you ready to make daily decisions that give you more joy?
- Is that joy pinging from your heart like sonar?
- Can others feel your solid truth with confidence?

- Can others feel you don't need validation because you know who you are?

This is living in "I" consciousness.

Anytime any external influences decide a truth to be good for you, view it as a "you" choice, not an "I" choice. They are deciding how "you" should live, and you are now being tasked with asking yourself, "Do I expand with this person's choice for me or not?"

In other words, whatever "they" do or don't do doesn't affect you either way. If it doesn't raise your consciousness, you don't have to participate. You do not judge, criticize, or even get angry anymore. You consciously acknowledge your truth, make a course correction, and keep moving.

There are times when I feel like I haven't moved at all, despite my earnest efforts to progress. Yes, it happens. I'm sure you have also had that feeling of pushing against a brick wall and getting nowhere. However, as soon as I acknowledge that it's okay to take a break, I find that the rest catapults me through all the things I've been working on in a single leap. This process is about learning to ebb and flow with your choices. It's about navigating life's ups and downs by consistently asking yourself if your actions align with your highest good. Mastering the ability to rest and reengage is such a powerful tool.

What's happening for each of us involves learning to incorporate new forms of education across all aspects of our lives and integrating simpler protocols. Being conscious of our truths allows us to create our personal hands-on learning style.

Society has become entangled in a system fixated on momentary, mending medications, which neglects to explore root causes in health and all other aspects of life. The one-pill approach proves insufficient for most, especially in achieving long-term relief from physical and emotional pain.

Contrastingly, our unique personalities hold energy blueprints wired into our nervous systems that are effective for self-healing when we consciously seek out that truth. It is a personal journey for each of us to unearth these solutions. Like researchers, we should continually ask questions whenever we feel unsettled in any prescription, medical or otherwise, that isn't solving our challenge.

I figured this out with food via the Keto diet. It's been the best for me for twenty years, and I feel the best eating that way. Well-meaning friends, family, and even a few health professionals have said, "Oh, that's not good for you," or "You need to eat more of this (or that)." When I took others' advice, I felt lousier than when I did what I knew worked for me when I felt my best. I also know those who feel terrible following the Keto lifestyle. Both of my kids are vegetarians! This is the difference between high and low vibe conscious choices, determining which ones empower each of us differently.

What behaviors do you accept to fit in that cater to others but don't feed your spirit and block your truth? Most places aren't Keto-diet friendly, so I must plan and prepare to live my way without expecting others to change. Are you planning your life intentionally for a massive consciousness step up for your highest good? This example is just with food, but the "one pill doesn't work for all" principle can apply to any topic you get blocked on.

What are you waiting for to make yourself feel better? It's up to each of us to pick ourselves. Are you where you want to be? Are you open to exploring new social groups and healing modalities, living in new locations, unlearning unhealthy love, and relearning new healthy love tools, new ways to raise your kids, and options to eat lighter, conscious saving, and investing, to name a few? Are you open to adapting your life to live how your heart sings?

Keep in mind life isn't about neglecting others. Instead, it is about prioritizing our needs and desires without passing judgment on others who may not simultaneously share the same needs. The key lies in understanding frequency – aligning with those whose energy matches ours in each moment. A mismatch of energy leads to friction and other low-frequency feelings and hinders the fulfillment of our needs. It's silly to think we need to change the other person. When we shine our lights, we must give others the time to adapt to our evolved selves. Taking on others' energy can drain us or fill us. So, it's crucial to be conscious of the lifestyle you are intent on living and not get pulled into others' pain drama.

Being conscious of our truth is our game changer. Our spirit guides us to truth through our hearts. Our truths lie beyond us and govern much more than what meets the eye. Only when we become conscious of its influence can we make a genuine change in ourselves. But how? Ask your heart! Again, sit silently and listen closely to those subtle whispers deep inside. They hold all the answers you seek.

We must all pay attention to our hearts' desires to make the most of this energy. One powerful and quick exercise to connect with our hearts is to close our eyes. Take three deep DMT breaths (breathe in for 9 counts, hold for 9 counts, breathe out for 9 counts), and then place a hand over your heart. Then, ask your heart what it needs the most right now, and trust the feeling or message that arises. This is being conscious.

Some days, life tends to pass in a blur. You get caught up in a rush and swept up in the flow of your past actions and beliefs. Are you moving in a direction that feels good in your heart? Are you taking daily actions that fill you with joy and inspiration, or are you living out of habit?

Whatever awakenings or realizations we have around these questions, there's always support for us through any changes we wish to make, ideas, habits, or ventures we want to try if they match our truth. When we shed the superficial, the burdens, and the beliefs that block us from being our true selves, we can truly shine like the lighthouses we are always meant to be.

EXERCISES

1. Check your heart. Are you filling it with joy? What can you do now?

2. Choose one: Willing, neutral, courageous, trusting, optimistic, understanding, forgiving, affirming, or loving. (circle the one you choose) Now, apply it to everything, every conversation, every person you experience all week.

BADASSERY EXTRA CREDIT TIP

Write down one truth you say to God and avoid saying to others but would love to express it.
This is your Truth, and it's time to start living this life you deserve.

15

Observing Yourself Experiencing

...

Are you observing what you experience in your life? I mean, everything you experience. From sitting in traffic and standing in lines at the post office to your boss's/kids'/spouse's attitudes? Are you observing your self-induced oppression? Are you able to see that you are the only one who can allow your oppression? For example, you're the only one who can let the attitudes around you affect you. I know what you're probably thinking: "I'm not the one creating this crap." This is a harsh reality to become aware of if you don't want to see it. It requires an open mind.

This is excellent news if you have the necessary open mind and are ready to regain control of your life! You are ready to allow the waves of change in frequency to wash your slate clean. This next phase is about who you choose to grow into instead of who you cut off.

What does changing our experiences mean? It means changing our beliefs about the experience. And what does changing our beliefs mean? It means we're empowered to change who we want to be, including the circle in which we choose to exist. So, everyone champions your growth, whether it's you at home resting or out climbing a mountain. Your tribe becomes more apparent, and you are less interested in explaining who you are and why. Who you are seeps out of your pores and pings out as a sonar vibration.

The more spiritually awake you become, the lighter you feel. When you feel lighter, your inner lighthouse shines; the darkness in your life is illuminated. That can be scary at times. Why? Because this new light now shows what you have put up with or what you have been unaware of. It's scary to wonder if you're capable of removing it from your life. It's become a bad habit. Even more challenging to understand is why we would be okay with holding onto unsupportive people, environments, and experiences. The brighter we become, the more vivid the things we have avoided are in our view.

Many still experience inner conflict due to old habitual patterns of helplessness. It's hard for some people to imagine that it's a choice (free will) to stay helpless instead of sovereign and free. Some, in this very moment, wouldn't dream of letting go of that with which they identify. Most don't even realize what unhealthy things they identify with are, in fact, causing their pain. That's their story of playing safe and small.

Here are a few examples.

Are you repeatedly discussing your complicated relationships? That's your story to gossip instead of looking at your contribution to the difficulties.

Your difficult children are not doing well? That's your story to live through them instead of choosing expansion for yourself. (By the way, when you decide to expand, your children will have a map to live free choices.)

Your spouse who isn't working and does nothing to grow? That's your story to play unlovable, enabler, or controller.

Your cycling sadness and anxiety? That's been your identity for maybe several lifetimes up until now. Does it feel good? Of course not. Guess what? This requires you to speak a new language to yourself and everyone else: "I'm a warrior, and I choose to expand."

WARNING! Your ego will fight hard to maintain these lack-mentality comfort zones learned in childhood. While you are miserable, it knows how to function with habitual behavior, keeping you in a loop of falling into ego control. It wants to be correct, it wants to protect you, and it fears change. The ego tricks you into repeating habitual, unwanted experiences! When the ego tells you, you don't deserve it, that is total bullshit! It's a simple choice to research how to get what you want on your own instead of staying uncomfortable until you are forced to make the change. You will make a change at some point because the universe will ensure it.

If you are habitually used to dark, depressing, and destructive patterns and habits, this empowered approach can be very tough. Emotions are not easy if you resist even seeing your harmful habits. It's as if you're blind to them.

Many, including you, your friends, and your family, may find themselves in hopeless situations. It may feel this way, but this is your moment! It would be best if you flipped like a coin. Flipping the coin means this is the exact situation you want to be in, because it gives you your power back. When you're under pressure, and the pressure pushes you to take a new step, let the old misery, sadness, and lack mentality wash it away.

If you feel hopeless, old programming and teachings are designed to work against you, not for you. They are designed to make you throw your hands up and say, "This is just what I'm going to live with… suffering, survival, and being miserable. I see no options at getting the things I want."

But those feelings are exactly what you are looking for. If you look at this doom and gloom feeling of despair as an opportunity to overcome, you will find the chance to shine.

Now are you observing your self-induced oppression? Are you allowing prolonged cruel or unjust treatment or control?

The following tool will give you your power back. I call it Observing Two Levels Above the Experience, or O2 for short. Let me explain how this works. Activate this one tool for the next month to grow and shine.

- Pick a habit or experience you are ready to wash away. Pick just one thing.
- Then, when you experience that thing, imagine you leave your body and observe yourself. Observe yourself doing that thing.
- Observe what your physical body is doing and allow it to be.

Don't absorb, and don't become the experience. Just observe it. And say, "Hmmm, this will be interesting to view how this experience can either get me into hot water, or I can seek a better way out or around it." Or you may get a chuckle out of it and push the experience, or boulder, out of your way now that you're finally done addressing it. You're free to see it as no longer part of you.

O2 Tip: remember, when you get stuck on a bad habit or belief, say to yourself, "Okay, it's O2 time." Start observing yourself, observing an experience. I named it this because I sometimes forget to be in observer mode. So, my short reminder code O2 is my go-to when I'm uncomfortable in an environment or situation. I start observing myself after saying go O2 to see you.

This means letting your spirit observe your mind and your body's experiences. Watch yourself as you would watch others in any social crowd. But you are watching how you do you. You have more control when observing vs. feeling environments and situations. Do you like how you show up? If not, you have the power within you to change.

EXERCISES

1. What repeating experience from your past no longer serves you?

2. Do you recognize patterns that you don't like but allow them to surface for observation and removal?

3. Can you observe others in triggered situations? What did you watch unfold?

BADASSERY EXTRA CREDIT TIP

Use this phrase to reset your habit: "I am powerful, creating my reality from my soul, not from my suffering." I observe from O2.

16

Rat Race Realization

...

It's time to wake up and make a conscious effort to remove ourselves from living in the rat race. Take the time to detach yourself from external sources of power -- that lurking sense of competition, trying to keep up with the Joneses, or being "on top" at work or school.

Detaching from external influences allows our genuine inner truth to shine through; it becomes exciting, invigorating, and just plain liberating! Even taking small steps toward self-discovery can bring great rewards. To learn our actual values and allow those values to guide our choices leads us closer and closer to achieving all we can become.

It's not only about seeing the scary truth externally. But our life's journey is about seeing our internal truths. Do you use your time to stop racing to where the external tells you and start to be your brightest truth?

You may not have even realized that we have been in a rat race for the last 50 or more years of our lives. You may have thought you weren't one of them. A little rat running on the same wheel day in and day out, chasing the elusive cheese. But now, when you look back, you can see the patterns you lived in, perpetuated by the screens you watched. They encouraged you to wake up, eat breakfast, get the kids ready for school, take them to school, go to work, eat lunch, pick up the kids, come home, make dinner, turn on the TV, and get indoctrinated with programming that intentionally wired our brains. These digital programs invested in many repeating topics to keep us smaller and less than others.

Then you went to sleep following the programming, which was integrated deep into your brain so that it was etched into the memory banks of your truth, only to wake up and do it again. Rarely does a person wake up and say, "This sucks! I don't want to repeat this perpetual Groundhog Day like everyone else!" and walk out the door to try something new. So many are blind rats, unaware we do it.

Not all of you were in a race. Those of you who broke the system before it revealed it needed to be broken…Congratulations! You are likely a realist who wanted to live your life with a more significant existence and who realized you were asked to live small and suffer unnecessarily. You recognized you wanted to live with freedom, no rules, and no restrictions on your truth. It's highly likely that you were then labeled as odd at that point.

This programming has lasted so long that most are upset because this rat wheel life is ending or being interrupted with Truth. These truth-seeking souls, being stubborn rule breakers, are who you can thank for your awakening. By getting off the rat wheel and finding more effortless ways to live, there is a door that opens leading to a more genuine way of expressing one's truth. It's meant to. If this chaos makes you uncomfortable, it's asking you to pay attention and look deeper for yourself. The odd souls lead you to free yourself from survival mode and start living.

The race is ending. The competition of who's more beautiful, who's more educated, who's more intelligent, more financially successful, built a more significant business, has a better body, has the best children, on and on and on - those races are over.

The emerging awareness is not to provoke distress about your growth potential as much as it is about releasing something significant, namely the element of competition.

Now more than ever, the only actual competition that exists (and has ever existed) is the one with yourself.

If you're still relying on the external digital wizards, as I describe them, like the wizard behind the curtain in the movie "The Wizard of Oz" or any mainstream media, turn it off! It's old-fashioned propaganda programming keeping you focused on the race from which you will not and cannot benefit.

The energy of the collective awakening has shifted from confining you to opening your mind, and the discomfort of the truth has forced you to go within. It is time to start to research and understand why your screens are not in your best interest. Why do "the wizards" not give you the power to heal, teach, invest, live, and create the life you deserve? This has been such a frustration for me most of my life. Why is the news, commercials, radio, and social media so full of drama and toxic trauma? It rarely, if ever, shows healing or suggests improving your life. It is simply the digital delivery of darkness and fear!

Remember, it is because the boxed system of wizards does not want you to be okay. "You're not okay, you're not okay, you're not okay," creates an internal storm inside of you that believes you need to reach outside of yourself to find a solution to be okay, as the screen has repeatedly told you.

As many of you have seen, the screens' solutions do not work. So, then what, you ask?

Get quiet and ask an essential question: What do I love, and how can I share my gifts with others? Each of us came here for our own truths, for our own higher purposes, because we are amazing and blessed in our spiritual and cellular DNA. We are awakening to our 5th Dimension consciousness. The 5th dimension is simple to understand. It's your spirit, it's your higher self, and it's your true self. If you sat knee to knee with your God and God asked if you are you living your true gifts and purpose in life, most immediately answer, "No." That's the 5th dimension of no time or space truth. It's just the truth without all the mind and body messiness.

The fastest solution I can give all of you is the "Zodiac Wheel is Your Medicine Wheel" course I teach. Look at your chart and see your specific personal areas to focus on healing and filling your soul with what it asks for, not what complete strangers suggest. *(View: Expansion page)*

I suggest you look at your astrological natal chart. It holds lessons awaiting completion. When you complete these weak spots, they will become the medicine you need to grow confidence, financial success, emotional abundance, love, children, communication, health, spiritual awakening, and joy.

But you have felt powerless because you have been told for a very long time to follow the screen and do what it tells you. It's simply amnesia - forgetting who you are. Your soul has a blueprint, which is your own personal user manual.

Those who listen to my weekly webinar and podcast, "Truth Tribe," know I have a massive issue with the external world telling you that you are not perfect.

Here's a question: What screen do you watch that tells you how amazing, powerful, and capable you are of healing yourself? What screen shows you the steps to be remarkable? Hmmmm, I can't think of a single mainstream institutional system, media, education, religious, financial, or government system that delivers self-empowerment products or programming ONLY. Where do you turn on THAT programming? This is total BS. If they won't tell you, I will. You have superpowers! We all do! It Is time we each became aware of them.

Your powerful self is a visual picture shown in your birth chart, an actual blueprint with all the tips and solutions to make your life more confident. The coolest part is that we chose this life.

We chose our life, parents, experiences, and personality. How could we have chosen this?

I get asked a lot … Why are these terrible things happening?

Spiritual Poverty. *(Not religion. That's a whole different topic of trying to control our interactions with God, or source energy. I find this whole middleman mumbo jumbo to talk to God silly, but hey, just my truth.)* By spiritual poverty, I mean the lack of spiritual connection to your truth and power. (*The lack of spiritual tools to connect to source consciousness.*)

Well, it starts with source energy…

1. God is source energy, the first layer. God is the highest of all unconditional love and creation. That is the first layer your soul decides to incarnate at this level into an earthly experience. You are a spark of light from God consciousness light.
2. The second layer is the consciousness in the Galaxy, which holds the planets and the planetary system. As you pass from soul source energy, you pass through the layer of planetary consciousness energy. You take on an imprint like a tattooed map on your soul. This is your personality in this lifetime or how you express yourself and how you think.
3. The third layer is Density consciousness. The soul then is born into the density consciousness from creation. Then, your spiritual tattoo blueprint of consciousness moves into the 3D form (a.k.a. human) as your internal GPS map to guide you.

Simplified version: Spirit, Mind, Body.

Your soul chose this date, this time, and this energy to come in and support the planet right now with its ascension to a higher frequency. This spirit frequency is already in your DNA. Remembering you are connected to source consciousness raises the frequency to a more loving state for an entire collective.

You are living at the most incredible time on earth, and you chose to live at this higher vibration. So, stop running the race. You are not a rat, you are not bad, you are not imperfect. You are pure source consciousness of love perfection with amnesia. Your soul knows what to do and how to live expansively. You have the map. USE IT. Your chart is holding the key.

Back to that medicine wheel, or your energy tattoo blueprint. That is where your medicine resides. Not out there… not from them. It is not external.

You are powerful, and I am so fed up with everyone waiting for someone else to tell them they will be OK. As scary as it might look, step into your truth, step into your karma, and step into your power.

Karma is not negative. Karma is not what you put out that comes back to you. Karma is about difficult topics for you, and you come to complete them (like a challenging subject in school). When you skip a rough patch and avoid it, what happens? It repeats and brings you back to shitty experiences again. It will continue to repeat and bring you these experiences because life is not happening to you to hurt you. Life is happening for you. You chose that blueprint to follow to finally wake up and see it as your own creation. When you do, you can complete it.

Recall from the introduction that Karma originates from "Kri," meaning "to do." Your karma boulders act like hot spots, sending signals prompting your attention towards challenges. Please recognize that you wield the power of a bulldozer to eliminate them. Acknowledge and tell yourself, "If I cease this or engage more in that, I'll feel better." Bingo! Medicine Wheel at your service. This is where healing lies in your hands, not the TV's screen.

You chose your blueprint to raise your consciousness to the 5th dimension quantum awareness, seeing Truth in all realities of your life.

Most people are upset because they have been programmed to live small and constricted lives. The age of Aquarius will not allow it. Open your mind to what your soul asks from you. How big can you dream, and how expansive can you imagine? I mean, unicorn shit…and dragons to unconditional love, immediate physical healing, emotional healing, success, and diseases like cancer eradicated. It's time to dream into your reality the concept of living your truth to the greatest expanded level.

EXERCISES

1. What better way could there be to start than by questioning: what is your particular rat race to which you have been blind?

2. Commit today towards being your lightest self and stepping into Your Truth completely. What will you do daily to live your inner soul's truth?

3. Do you know your birth chart? Use the EXPANSION page to get the link to print your chart and take the zodiac wheel course to understand yourself more today.

BADASSERY EXTRA CREDIT TIP

Are you more upset that you're playing small or afraid to play BIG?

This is the best time in history to do it.

Go BIG! That's where we're going, so why wait?

EXPANSION CHAPTER 16

Zodiac Wheel is Your Medicine Wheel Course
available on my website
ideserveitnow.com/courses

Free Astrology Wheel located at
ideserveitnow.com/tools
for full chart description.
(Learn your hot spots and your life purpose)

17

Relationships Are Revealing You

...

Your relationships reveal you! Okay, chapter complete!

I feel like a broken record listening to myself on how often I discuss this topic. You are the designer of your life. This concept was hard for me to accept as well, until I got honest with myself. I attracted into my life the frequency of the sonar I emitted, much the way a submarine navigates the dark ocean in search of other subs. Like submarines sending out vibration signals to locate objects, when the ping matches the vibration of another sub, bingo, they pinpoint its location on their radar.

So, how do your relationships reveal you? The simple way to figure this out is to skip over the easy, likable, joyful people in your life and jump right to the irritating relationships. They are in your life to wake you up. Yes, this is the time to send them a little thank you in your mind. Yes, they are a gift alerting you to remove that boulder.

Reviewing the reality of your relationships is the fastest way to do a self-awareness check. What relationship has the biggest stranglehold on you?

Everything in this life is about relationships and how you raise your consciousness in them.

Relationships are not just with people, they are also reflections of your health, finances, friends, family, career, security, body image, material things, food, intimacy, communication, spirituality, and intuition.

Everything is in a direct and deep relationship with you. It is up to you to wake up to the relationship you want to have versus the one you currently have.

I know you didn't come here to be mediocre, to be small, to use another's map, or to fill up someone else's blueprint above yours, to believe their journey has more truth and value than yours.

You are a badass, beautiful soul, incarnated to ignite your free will to live a high-consciousness life. You came here to learn that heaven and earth are in your mind. And, in every reality you choose to immerse yourself in, you have free will to choose heaven. As you recall, you also have the free will to choose hell or experience hell just once and then repeatedly go back for visits.

You have complete power to live the truth you want, and it is your free will to choose you. Selflessness has been programmed in you for so long that you have forgotten the relationship with yourself is the place to find heaven on earth. God, source, has given you codes in your DNA to live your best life. Utilizing discernment involves recognizing that your purpose is to embody Christ-like qualities, not to diminish yourself, surrender, or endure suffering for any deity. It's about transcending martyrdom and breaking free from repetitive cycles of hardship. This extends beyond sacrificing yourself solely for another human or aligning with programming found in various doctrines like those centered around health, wealth, love, and life. No doctrine on the planet is wrong or right. It is simply guidance for finding your relationship within. Who are you, and is that person you are being who you choose to be forever more? Christ spent his life until his 20s learning from master healers. He wasn't just magical; his powers didn't just one day arrive. He learned how to discipline his gifts that you also hold. He was a man who mastered his badassery skills.

If you're repeatedly told to give up yourself for others in the wrong context, it will always feel like you give all your energy, time, and things away and never receive the balance in return. But the ocean tide that goes out must come back in, just like the unattended garden inside you needs nourishment.

Why, then, would so many come to earth to have poor relationships with mindset, money, intimate relationships, health, security, and family challenges?

Why are we so focused on watching others making free-will choices that look ugly and destructive instead of focusing on what is best for each of us? Because we have been numb for a long time until now.

All this shifting of consciousness is a gentle tap of slow drip awakening to our Christ-like powers. I'm not making religious or political statements. I encourage finding the truth inside yourself to live with the same power as Jesus was expected to live by embodying

God consciousness. Christ-like refers to shining your talents like Christ with love. Learn how to heal yourself, charge your water to love water (Expansion), detox your body into clean cells, teach yourself to fish, garden, move, and think from your truth and not from some unknown source that does not want you off their system of sleepwalking (a.k.a. rat wheel control).

Instead of being upset with others in their destructive states, it's time to see them in a state of sleepwalking and nothing more. They will trip and fall on a lesson they have chosen to awaken to on their own.

Everyone is living from their place of consciousness. If you're upset with someone's actions, you view them from your disappointment that they don't want to expand into higher consciousness. Or they don't want to come down to your drop in lower consciousness. It's all you. They are just being them.
What the collective is experiencing right now is the awakening of their truth, and it looks like this: a

repetitive tapping on your third eye to get you to see beyond what your numbed-down mind has been ignoring for so long. The universe is tapping on your intuitive mind to give you an expanded observing perspective.

What is the Third Eye?

It's the point on your forehead, precisely centered above the bridge of your nose, resembling an actual eye that is not physically visible. Yet, its purpose is to observe the unseen. Intuition and awareness. It observes energy instead of physicality. This is the most significant awareness you can learn to nourish. When observing things, do you focus on their energy, physical presence, or language? Consider this example: if you don't speak French, individuals who do might use any name without causing you distress; you're simply observing their presence rather than their words. Using your intuition is like seeing energy instead of the words or actions you dislike.

Your awakening is a repetitive tapping on your frontal cortex, igniting your pineal gland. Whenever you see an awareness that scares you, it's simply meant to get your attention. Each external relationship that frustrates you awakens you to see your internal imbalance. Each unsettled interaction balances YOU. Although, it may seem likes it's a dispute or frustration for both of you, it's for you to see what you are aligned with, and not necessarily to balance the other person.

It's time to stop carrying others' BS boulders around. It's time to up your relationship game, not lower it.

Whether single, married, or in a committed partnership, it's time to be crystal clear about who you are and who you want to be (especially if you are not who you want to be). It's time to invest in a higher state of being every single day. Such clarity requires discipline. Find the education you need to live your soul's truth.

Each time some undesired "thing," experience, or person gets your attention, it's tapping your Third Eye to become more awakened.

Relationships reveal what we came to master. Relationships trigger us to see what we may be avoiding. What topic is continually tapping you awake? It does not have to be a person. You are in a relationship with ALL things; some things you excel with and some not. What is it for you? Health, happiness, security, safety, trust, fear, guilt? What is your relationship with those emotions?

If you say you don't know what areas you avoid seeing as your growth point, you're simply imprisoning yourself, and it's a cop-out of your truth. Your relationships won't know to evolve until you speak it. The universe can't assist in guiding you to new, healthier relationships until you are clear on your intention.

I'm not talking about just an intimate love relationship. As I mentioned above, ALL relationships. Those in business, health, and career are all up for grabs. Does it feel good? At first, it's likely to be uncomfortable. Again, this takes discipline and practice, like any other skill (walking, reading, etc.)

I hear so many excuses why people cannot have what they want. We are continually being pulled into "lack" mentalities or beliefs, and, as you all know, you can go down with it or break free.

Releasing certain elements may initially feel like it creates a void or emptiness. Yet, this void acts as a vacuum, yearning for expansion. Consider this an opportunity to grow something new that aligns with your newfound clarity. This is the time for you to ask yourself better relationship questions.

EXERCISES

1. What relationships reveal your resistance to releasing unhealthy habits? What is your weakest relationship right now? Health, wealth, love, lack, learning, dreams?

2. How does this look in real-life experiences? Where do you hide a part of yourself and wish to be free to live in peace?

3. In what relationship do you shrink and play small instead of living your best life, no matter anyone's opinion?

BADASSERY EXTRA CREDIT TIP

How aware of your selfishness or unselfishness are you? Are you needy or the doormat?

EXPANSION CHAPTER 17

LOVE WATER

Repeated from an earlier chapter.

18

ASTROLOGY LOST IT'S WOO WOO

...

For twenty years, I kept my talent, connecting astrology blueprints to success coaching, hidden out of fear that peers wouldn't believe in its power. I'll admit that I have been labeled 'woo-woo' more than once, and I was scared it would make people doubt my ability to be a fantastic coach who could empower anyone by revealing the truth about their worthiness. Then, one day, it hit me: who cares what others think? If understanding someone's birth chart can help them uncover their strengths and take control over their challenges, this is a tool worth using!

If we see where our opportunities lie within ourselves by looking into our blueprints, we can take back control of living fully instead of shrinking out of fear.

No more victim mentality or pointing fingers. Seeing others clearly takes courage – which thankfully runs deep throughout us all but sometimes needs activation.

There's nothing quite like being true to yourself and helping others. From millennials making millions from their T-shirt businesses to inspired moms running successful New Earth Schools that focus on teaching validation of truth instead of memorization, the potential for self-expression is infinite!

You could be a teacher, healer, builder, accountant, surgeon, or artist. The possibilities are endless when you focus your energy on living according to what feels right in your heart and chart versus what you think the world wants you to do.

I know living with such clarity and confidence feels scary, because we believe we don't have a handbook on how to live our new reality and higher-consciousness life without a map.

NEWSFLASH! The truth is we each have user manuals! They aren't one-size-fits-all either. It's yours and only yours because you are perfect.

Let me be clear. Astrology and planets are not your excuses to live with less. They are your map to teach you how to remove detours that keep you from your dreams.

What if you know which relationships are your weak points but aren't able to see the big picture to heal them? They keep repeating it, and you keep missing it. If you know what hamster wheel you continue to run on, only to stay imprisoned in the same unwanted experiences, this is due to you wanting to please others instead of yourself. This is also because we hope it's the external world's fault instead of our own for repeatedly accepting unsavory experiences. Your soul knew you would avoid these uncomfortable situations, so in a sense, your soul chose a blueprint to assist you by setting boulders in your way to further your growth.

It goes back to the Jesus syndrome I have referenced. You didn't come here to be Jesus. You came here to learn to love yourself and offer healing to others by using your gifts to teach them "how to fish," not to fish for them. Evolution is happening, and you're on this train whether you like it or not. The universe keeps sending you messages to take care of yourself, so you have more to give to the group when needed.

This will not happen if you are the only one giving and not receiving. God gave you free will to say, "Yes, that behavior you attract in your spouse, boss, friend, or child is not Christ-like. Heck, it's downright embarrassing that you accept such drama."

It's all about stating, "I'll go where I can be more my authentic self. If I miss the bullseye, I will make changes in myself. I will change my energy so I can attract upgraded experiences."

If you keep finding yourself on wishy-washy dates, you are being wishy-washy. If your spouse keeps arguing, you keep showing up to fuel your inner rage. If you keep financing your friends or lovers only to be used, you are being a doormat and hoping they will stop stepping on you. Stop this BS! It is time to raise your awareness, learn how to know yourself, and grow your self-worth. This is all about you. What you don't like is that you need to step up and say, "FUCK NO! I'm out! Show me my map to change me."
(EXPANSION PAGE)

EXERCISES

1. What are your weak spots on your astrological birth chart? Top 4?

2. How does finding out the challenges you came to master at birth help you?

3. Check your chart for your Moon, Saturn, North Node, and Chiron to see your most enormous boulders? Circle them, research them, and decode their lessons for your life.

BADASSERY EXTRA CREDIT TIP

Take the course *Zodiac Wheel is Your Medicine Wheel.*

EXPANSION CHAPTER 18

Print and learn Your Zodiac Birth Chart.

Print The Winning Wheel
to see what areas of your life need attention.

19

DOES THE "F" WORD UPSET YOU?

...

I'm sure most of you think I'm referring to one "F" word in particular. You know, the one that I often express when I'm excited about a topic. But I can think of a few "F" words that upset many.

What F word upsets you the most? Fuck or Freedom?

Why do we get stuck in language? Because of the value and context, we attach to it.

Labels are such a big deal lately. When we refrain from using labels as judgements to define people, we can better understand their unique personal energy expression. It's why some hear the "F" word and think it's a trashy, vulgar word, and others hear it as an adjective, a descriptor, or even an enhancement, as I do.

I was listening to Kevin Hart's audiobook on my road trip a few weeks ago. Because he's so funny, and his energy and consciousness are so high, I didn't even hear how often he used the "F" bomb. You feel so good laughing with him that his energy transmutes any words into high consciousness.

Then, when you hear an angry, victim-state, low-consciousness person speak, it sounds low and heavy. When I say WTF, no one gets too bothered because you know I'm saying it as an expression with no malicious intent.

However, when I speak about the other "F" word, FREEDOM, this gets people upset. In private coaching discussions, when I ask, "What does the word 'free' make you feel?" Clients are more triggered by "free" than when I use the other "F" word.

Fuck isn't weird to them, but freedom, or lack of it, is! It's their context of the word. Freedom, when I show them how they always had it and just need to express it, often ignites the other "F" word. "FUCK! That pisses me off that I didn't see it before!"

Fascinatingly, when low-vibration TV wizards say your freedom is being limited, it sounds scary and something to be afraid of. Many are willing to accept some stranger's context of freedom or lack thereof, not considering who the wizard is. Consider your sources. Are they a high or low vibe? Ask who delivers the message from behind the curtain?

Do you walk out the door and adjust your sails to think differently than the wise old wizard of Oz? Not once was my freedom restricted during the entire pandemic promoted as fear on every digital device possible because my consciousness was to thrive, not to survive.

It's time for you to walk outside and ask, "How can I create my independence and personal freedom? How can I stay sovereign and independent? I have always had it, as Glinda the Good Witch told Dorothy, or Daune, my truth teacher, has been telling me." You are the director of your own movie. You've been free all along. Stop listening to low-consciousness wizards.

The cool part is that we are shifting to higher frequencies, because we can see the freedom question surfacing in our consciousness, personally and globally. Wizards say you are not free to live as you choose. And many of us are saying, "F You! Watch me!"

- What context does freedom have for you?
- Are you free to choose your values? Yes.
- Are you free to choose your friends? Yes.
- Are you free to choose your health? Yes.
- Are you free to choose your spending, eating, beliefs, and faith? Yes, you are!

- Are you free to have courage? Yes, today and every day.

Choose courage with every interaction and watch your consciousness shift from words to vibes to visuals.

Do you determine how you live your life, or do you give your life to others to determine what you can and cannot do? Do you even realize you can choose freedom? Do you need to shift to a higher consciousness to live a freer life?

You only need to readjust your sails, not the destination. What end destination do you want? What does it require you to do to get there?

This is why I have shared repeatedly that it's time to love your inner truth and who you are inside, and research all the things that scare you outside and hold you back from living that truth.

Ask yourself, "Do I realize my freedom is not determined by what any low-consciousness wizards, friends, employers, or strangers say or want for me?"

Can you look for roads where you are free to heal, live, spend, talk, and be who you want to be at any time?

It would be best if you first chose higher-consciousness beliefs. Truth to thoughts to things means those truths must be at the core of your valued beliefs. Then, find all those who are in the same belief's tribe.

When you listen to anyone speak from today on, listen to them as a programmed person and consider where they got the words they are delivering to you. Who is the source of those words? What is the reason they want you to hear those words? Are they freedom words or fearful words?

If, at any time, some random wizard behind the curtain tells you what is and is not true, you will KNOW when you simply ask yourself, "Is this my core truth?" How will you know? It will not feel high vibe or true if it's not delivering freedom. So, it won't be true for you. Even if you don't have proof that it's true, you can feel it restrict your ability to move freely.

Then, ask, dig, and find a high-consciousness truth, person, or environment that gives you the "F" word: FREEDOM. What do you need to know to make it a yes for you to be free?

DO NOT ACCEPT NO! No requires knowledge. You "know" what you need to convert your no to a yes.

- What does freedom look like for you?
- What would moving look like if you lived in the city and it didn't allow you easy access to what you needed to be free to live as you choose?

- If you live with kids and you need to be free to teach *them* how to be free and independent in a new school, where would it be located?
- What steps might you take if you have a spouse from whom you need to feel free in your marriage without ending it?
- If you have poor health and need to access new health paradigms to be free from the misuse of medicine, who do you know with excellent health and could ask for a resource to shift?
- What would you do if you had a career that only paid your bills but shackled you and held you back instead?

TWO STEPS TO CHECK CONSCIOUS AWARENESS:

1. Start with one area of your life that needs to be free. Have the courage to find a way to be F'ing Free. Turn off all digital wizards who are telling you to be scared.

2. Research your zodiac sign's challenges, and you'll see it's likely a weak spot in your life. Check your moon sign and Saturn to help you see yourself. (EXPANSION-Free Birth Chart)

Our personalities have two fears I see repeatedly: rejecting or restricting freedom. If your personality fears being rejected, Fuck might be a word that upsets you by rejecting others who may use it to express freedom. If you fear being restricted, Freedom (or lack of it) will disturb you.

You're now being given a chance to raise your frequency to a higher consciousness, and your soul knows it. You chose to be here at this time in history to live this experience for a reason. It's for sure not to be in Fucking Survival mode.

Step into it and see how fucking beautiful your life can be when you are in power. Stop giving your fucking freedom to people you will never know, and whose nontruths you would never want from the start.

You choose your reality.

Criticism or Caring: no matter the language spoken, what is the consciousness of the person delivering it? Do not live another day without raising your consciousness and scanning theirs for how it affects you (not how to change them).

It isn't about the words fuck or freedom; it's about if you choose to live in a conscious state of being that isn't affected by any word or person externally. Your energy will dictate your life. Can you choose freedom and thrive in every action?

Your view of the world shows you the reality of what you consider good and evil. When life pushes you, are you fearful and thus using your programmed language, or do you choose to live in a free state?

How you live is not a language but a consciousness vibration state. Your life will reflect your choice to live in a controlled language or with a caring consciousness.

You have a supercomputer in your hand for the majority of the hours of your day. You no longer have an excuse for why you don't research ways to be free from anything that ever challenges you again.

EXERCISES

1. "F" words are no different than S, C, or any injustice you believe is wrong. Can you choose to see life through loving eyes? Which "F" word triggers which emotions in you? Why?

2. Base of Consciousness delivery. What does it feel like to share a Caring versus Critical delivery?

3. Yes or No? Do you dig and research for freedom to override your fear? "Fuck this (old way of being/doing/thinking)!" is your new freedom mantra.

4. Do NOT accept NO. Raise your consciousness and scan theirs. Is this person in your highest good?

5. Do you use your supercomputer to research ways to free yourself from suffering?

BADASSERY EXTRA CREDIT TIP

Do you ignore a person's language because you feel their higher consciousness makes you raise yours?

EXPANSION CHAPTER 19

Print and learn the Zodiac Birth Chart
Look for Saturn and Moon descriptions.
See if these two areas of your life need attention.

20

POWER TOOLS COME IN MANY FORMS

...

Growing up in the Catholic religion never made any sense to me. I was raised by an incredible mother and grandmother who didn't draw a line between religious and spiritual guidance. Religion and spirituality were interchangeable. They all pointed to God.

My Catholic grandmother would take me to church to light prayer candles for loved ones. Afterwards, she would read playing cards like tarot, seeing them as representations of the cardholders' energy. She interpreted the cards as messages based on their energy patterns. Each card had a number, and numbers were significant to her as they composed the universe. Though she may not have described it this way, she used her intuition and spiritual gift in this simple yet profound practice. I doubt that's how she would describe it, but that's what she was doing. It's so funny how simple it is.

So, when I ask you to consider how you feel about crystals, astrology, Angel Cards, Tarot, Reiki, psychics, pendulums, dowsing, etc., do you get uncomfortable?

- What do these topics mean to you?
- Who taught you what to believe about them?
- Are they in conflict with your indoctrinated beliefs?

Very likely, the ones you were raised with or taught in Sunday school or religious education classes.
Now, for a moment, redirect your thoughts to the electric current in the walls of your home. That electricity supplies the power to warm rooms, cook food, read, and light up the darkness. Return to your thoughts about spirituality, religion, or faith, all of which empower, feed, nurture, and enlighten your

mind and soul. Guess what? Both power supplies are the same but use different tools. Power tools. You're directed back to energy every time.

Throughout time, we've always known things match their energy frequency, no matter what tool we use. Regardless of religions, doctrines, cards, psychics, etc., all hold love and information as well as disinformation and control. It's up to you to find the blessings instead of the fears.

When you consider the metaphysical tools listed above, ask yourself how they make you feel energetically. Do you feel weird or guilty because friends or relatives labeled those items and people who use them as bizarre by shaming them?
Ask yourself: What does a crystal, a unique rock, really mean to you?

Is it because you were told they were bad in conjunction with your controlled box religion, and if you used them to heal your energy, that you were a sinner?

Were you ever instructed to avoid unconventional approaches while being discouraged from questioning the rationale behind teachings that label everyone as sinners? Moreover, were you expected to surrender your last pennies to the collection jar so you could feel less miserable by giving them to others? Nothing seems more unloving than kicking someone when they are down, as many religious boxes are known to do.

Condemning any of the above list, religious, spiritual, or metaphysical, keeps you in a box of enslaved, controlled, "lack" beliefs. Astrology, for example, is another language that has been used since before Mesopotamia. It was used to grow crops and navigate the oceans. Something as simple as a planet directs the power back into you to connect to Source-God consciousness. And, if you choose to connect to your

God on your own, you don't need a "box" or a middleman telling you how to live free and in love. We lost our way many thousands of years ago and now are in a window of time showing us how to reconnect to Source consciousness, unconditional love, which is God consciousness. And no box, book, or human can do that for you. You must pull your head up, awaken, and use any tool or resource possible to tap into that power within you that reminds you of your omnipresent, God-conscious love.

I believe any doctrine that dictates you are a sinner wants control over how you see yourself. It's easy to feel helpless and dependent on others, like a beggar, when you hand your power to someone else. But it's important to remember that you are capable of saving yourself. You have the power to shape your own life and choose your own path. Not the life you were told you had to live from a box, a book, or a person. So, I ask you to do as I did as a kid. Start asking yourself how does this box, book, crystal, or human make you feel? If it is that of a sinner, lack or less, find a new tool to access God. Lighten up and have a little fun with this!

To tap into the consciousness of love, you must be aware of the love within yourself. You are pure love and must see the inner child within you who deserves that pure love. Today is your day to choose a tool (or several) and a simple phrase to reassure your inner child.

1. Imagine your younger self: Visualize a younger version of yourself standing before you.
2. Visualize picking up little you and hug your inner child: Envision yourself reaching out, picking up your younger self, and embracing them tightly. Say to yourself:
   "I got you, Little _____ (insert your name)."
3. Add: "I am The BOSS Of Me, and we are free. I'm God's love!"

EXERCISES

1. What is one belief you were taught when you were young that feels untrue today?

2. Now that you're aware of that non-truth, what would you say to Little You to reassure him/her?

BADASSERY EXTRA CREDIT TIP

Take a field trip to a crystal shop and check out what attracts you to it. Then, research the qualities it holds and if they resonate with you.

21

Your Parents' Marriage Mirage

...

You married your parents! Yes! Can you believe it? You dated them, and you married them. You designed the whole thing. It's one of the most challenging realities to accept and would seem like the easiest to understand how we replicate what we were taught: good, bad, and ugly.

In 30 years of teaching and training, I have found one common theme and truth in relationships. We were not only taught how to live our lives in an educational setting, but we were also taught how to love by our parents. So, if humans are organically wired to co-create and seek out love, it's a no-brainer that we would learn and use the love we learned in our first home-based classroom.

The tricky part is that love has been hijacked from an energy or feeling to an action or behavior. From infancy to approximately ten years old, our first school is any adults in our environment. We are taught to love as they love. Such love was delivered in many forms in addition to positive emotions: control, guilt, shame, anger, abuse, abandonment, neglect, etc.

As I've been asked to help hundreds of clients improve their relationships through the years, I used a simple tool to reveal what kind of love they learned. It was often like a spiritual awakening when they saw they were repeating their parents' behaviors in their own relationships.

It was as if these clients, more often than not, married or dated one or both of their parents. Now, this is the part when adult temper tantrums happen. The ugly argument couples have often included phrases such as "You're acting like your mother" or "You're just like your father." The truth is, yes, you are, unconsciously.

Why do we date partners similar to our parents? The simple answer is that's all your nervous system knows. See it as less of a red flag and more of a growth opportunity. Then, use your unhealthy love programming as the lesson it was meant to be. That lesson is a catalyst to seek out a new, healthier version of love. Now, speak, write, act, and live as you prefer to rewire your nervous system from unhealthy love into a healthy version. Remember that this rewiring is only possible if you are invested in growing out of the "blame game" and into the catalyst's blessing.

So often, when couples have challenges, they don't necessarily need therapy. They must see that they married their parents and their parents' version of love. Seeking to feel love again as an adult, you reenact the feelings you experienced as a child. As we all know, not all of your childhood love was healthy, and this is where love gets unnecessarily messy. The simple solution is to ask whether you want your partner's parents' marriage. Does your partner want your parent's marriage? If you can ask that money question at the beginning, middle, or end of your relationship, you will have a chance to have healthier conversations that are less about what you aren't getting and more about what you want.

When you fall into unhealthy love patterns resembling your parents' influence, you will be able to say, "This is not what I want to bring to the table. My behavior/language/tone does not create a badass marriage." Ownership begins to build that power-couple energy because you are both in power, not neglecting the elephant in the room.

When all couples meet, each person enters as a whole and an individual. Then they fold into each other, forgetting to keep their confidence and power. You keep your confidence and power by owning what you bring in and what you don't want to deliver to your partner from your parents' influence.

Unlearning is unnerving. Loving yourself is the ultimate plan. Loving yourself is seeing the unhealthy love patterns you dragged around for years into your marriage or partnerships and then blamed them for not loving you enough to unload your unwanted baggage. No one is to blame for dragging around your old baggage but you. If you don't see it, you will keep fighting an elusive demon that doesn't exist. This is your simple "get out of jail free" card.

Once you see the lessons from your childhood that discouraged self-love, it opens your willingness to release what you learned in that "unloving home environment." This fosters a desire to thrive in your adult life. It is hard to imagine you have been programmed to accept an institutional mindset during your most influential years. Yes, you were in mental and emotional jail. You were taught to accept a jail of unhealthy love habits.

Yet, physical jails are one of the least programmed institutions in our society. Jails are less invested in taking away your mental powers. You can choose to read and learn whatever you want, and it's often what your soul is drawn to.

But you didn't pay attention to how you willingly accepted the small box programming at home and in schools, medicine, government, religions, digital screens, or even from total strangers. Do they have your highest good in mind, or theirs?

It's time to see if you are waking up to a decision: stay in their mental jail or walk away toward your truth. Your parents' "love jail" is riddled with limiting beliefs and actions given to them when they were young. They, too, had limited information to understand how to create healthy love. We can't place blame on them. We must use them as our springboards, our catalysts, to redefine the true capabilities of relationships and love for ourselves.

This is all done by three tools:

1. What marriage did my parents have, and do I want that same marriage? Why or why not?
2. Am I drawn to people or married to someone who recreates that same relationship for me now?
3. What marriage or relationship do I want instead, and what must I do to create that relationship?

Success in your relationship is more effortless when you remove your blame on others for why you "can't have the relationship you desire." You become a magnet when you express the traits of the healthy love you desire. So often, we don't realize this because no institution or environment has taught us how to learn healthy love. In essence, we are parched and starved for love, only to believe a version of unhealthy love when it shows up as the real thing, like a mirage in the desert. We imagine it is, or can be, what we starve for, which is healthy love.

Today is your day to evaluate your relationship. You have to be brutally honest about what you want and what you bring to the relationship that isn't what they or you deserve.

EXERCISES

1. What top 3 characteristics of your parents' marriage do you look for in your partner to give to you and that they may resist because it's your unconscious need to recreate unhealthy love?

2. What parts of your parents' marriage were healthy, and which do you want to recreate?

3. What are you afraid to say to your partner because it may hurt their feelings?
   If you say you don't want to be like your mother/father anymore (but that is the trait they sought in you), are you withholding a message in fear that they will not love you anymore?

4. What kind of marriage or partnership do you want to build with your spouse or partner?

BADASSERY EXTRA CREDIT TIP

If you are brutally honest with the parts of your parents' marriage you dislike, can you see where you bring that to your marriage out of habit and have not even been aware of it until now?

EXPANSION CHAPTER 21

Print Marriage Mission on Expansion Page
(use for marriage, dating, or singles to create clarity)

22

TRUTH TRUMPSTRASH

...

Old truths are disappearing, leaving a wake of confusion. "Lack" mindsets are products of past energy on Earth. However, they must surface for us to acknowledge, address, and release them for us to exist in higher consciousness. Old approaches, for example, shame or fear, aren't working in 5D energy. What is 5D energy? It's a 5th dimension where there is no time or space. The etheric, or non-physical, space is similar to when you meditate. You're not here, and you're not in your thoughts; you're in your dreams.

If I had a quarter for every time, I heard the phrase "When will we get there?" I'd be a gazillionaire. That very question is why you are not where you want to be. "There" implies a future destination, but here-and-now is all that exists. Many of you have been in a get-to-the-end mindset for so long that you miss life right in front of you. Your mindset has become so distorted trying to get somewhere. Often, you are not even aware of your daily surroundings. We are already "there." Understand, it's not a *place* you are trying to move *to.* Instead, "there" is a now *feeling* you learn to *embody*.

Here are some mindset examples. The Universe doesn't care if you swear. The Universe doesn't care if you fuck up. The Universe doesn't care if you call someone a name. The Universe doesn't care if you don't like the pain you're in and you're angry about it. The Universe doesn't care if someone is mean to you or makes you feel unimportant.

What the Universe does care about is if you correct course and start living your own damn truth. The Universe cares that you chose to be a specific puzzle piece in this lifetime, and you now choose to shine during this journey on Earth. You came to fulfill a specific mission. You're here because you've awakened from the old, negative bullshit programming that shrouds the legitimacy and honesty of spiritual truth. THIS is the mindset of "there."

Many of you are very stuck in old, indoctrinated, programmed "truths" and are going to struggle with this for a while. It's OK. Your soul knows what to do. Here are a few more examples.

Spiritually: If you're stuck in old, religious programs that preach you're a sinner, you're bad, or you're not enough, especially compared to one man who walked the Earth thousands of years ago, that's nonsense. One in particular taught you how to be Christ "like," meaning kind and confident in who you are and what gifts you are here to share, not to be a victim and suffer until you die, and that he will save you after a lifetime of martyr behavior.

Physically: If you're stuck in one method of healing that isn't working, this is also a bullshit belief. You are smart enough to figure out that you are an organic being. Maybe research the natural healing route by simply exploring alternatives to the current failed modality that exists rather than leaving your fate to someone else who is less invested in you and your health. Organic natural solutions will appear.

Mentally: If you are stuck in a lack mentality that says you must suffer a daily 9-5 grind, exhausted, with no time or energy left to thrive, that's also BS. If you struggle to pay your debt because you weren't born into a wealthy lifestyle and then told you wouldn't ever be financially secure and free, call bullshit! We ALL know people who have and live happy, successful lives that started from a negative place.

We each came here to fulfill our roles in the blueprint we chose (our individual birth charts). There is a badass inside of each of us waiting to let that soul out of jail.

Let's talk about jail, also known as your personal trash. I mentioned mental and emotional jail in the last chapter regarding relationship mindsets, essentially personal trash, or how we were programmed.

We have all been in jail for some time, real or imagined. It's right in front of us to see if you are ready to let go of any restrictions or feel blocked, frozen, or indecisive on how to move forward. Move anyway. Trust anyway. Believe anyway. We are all shapeshifting, and it's in our DNA to know where to find the open doors and the groups with whom to connect. Remember, we each came here for a very specific, purposeful journey and specific souls with whom to shift on that journey.

If past relationships have blueprints that no longer fit into the soul group in which you need to evolve, then they will not stay with you. Moving away from one another has nothing to do with you or them. It's completely each person's journey. As hard as this may seem at first, don't take a separation personally. Their actions, staying or leaving this earth plane, have nothing to do with not wanting to be with you, loving you, or desiring to evolve with you. Everything they do is precisely what they are here to do to be part of this consciousness evolution. There is no such thing as an accident, even if it is not a choice you would have made for them or a choice you would want them to have in your life experience.

I am here to inspire truth and emotional enlightenment. Both are very unstable on the planet at this moment. I know my role to play in this lifetime, and it is to show you an easier path to Spirit without the fucking rules and numbing of your souls. Here's a HUGE truth: your feelings are your superpower! If you feel it, trust it. If it feels like crap externally, it's crap. If a person, place, or experience makes you feel heavy and imprisoned, it is, in fact, CRAP. If you feel like crap internally, go there, look at it, and clear your crap. You will stop attracting external crap because you will no longer match that crappy frequency. It's no one's fault you came to be a warrior. Get your shovel out, clear the crap, and continue on your way.

Every pain and emotion, like fear or angst you experience, is meant to help you get out of it.

In other words, you cannot shift anywhere (start a new business, for example) if you hold onto or avoid how scared you are of failing (i.e., stuck standing in emotional trash). Yes, fear smells gross, and no one likes it. Yet, ignoring the fear (trash) only makes it smellier and lasts longer until you see it in your own life. Clearing yourself is like "taking out the trash." Acknowledge your fears, affirming that you deserve a better life. Commit to push through these emotions and gain clarity on environments that resonate with your inner lightness.

No one taught you to question the bullshit programs you have learned for thousands of years. No one taught you to question why we are simply accepting mindless madness that does not serve our souls. It's time to plug your nose, see the trash, grab a bag to pick up your inner shit and decide to throw it out. Burn the crap you have become used to accepting in your familiar lives. It's time to see you have allowed digital and societal wizards to numb you to that smelly trash. It is okay to admit you don't actually like it. You don't have to accept it! Accepting a numbing narrative is why so many have not changed until now.

You have filled a dumpster with years of bullshit, jumped in, and accepted what you've been "educated" to believe is true, instead of questioning it. It's no longer an option to live in a numb and imagined jail mode. You are not in jail. You are not in a dumpster. See your inner trash and replace it with patience, kindness, and love to live healthier and more unrestricted. No need to be sad or angry. Be aware that you are not compatible at the cellular level anymore.

To simplify, not living your truth is creating your anxiety. Are your current beliefs about health, wealth, love, money, God, and abundance what you deserve? Your puzzle piece is no accident. Neither is the addict, the healer, the mom, the bricklayer, the truck driver, or the quantum physicist. Their roles are all necessary. Your role is to see the truth. Let the wizard's victim words of fear and imprisonment die now. It's time to be who you are and stop trying to get somewhere you think is better. "There" doesn't exist, as discussed in the last chapter. Only here and now matters. Be who you came to be in the collective evolution.

See TRUTH right here, right now, and do not wait for a commercial to ask you if you feel sick. It's easy to pick a poison (or all sorts of poisons) to avoid your purpose on this planet. Drugs, alcohol, shopping, sex, food, over-exercising, over-giving, and people-pleasing are all distractions so you can avoid learning the truth about how to be free of the things that numb your soul.

If you've lost your job, a family member or friend, or a relationship, it's necessary for you to go to the next level of your evolution. Your soul has asked to move up the ladder in a sense. The anxiety you feel stems from your unwillingness to let go of what is no longer suitable for you.

So, your soul guides you into the darkest and smelliest part of the dumpster to get your attention to see a truth with which you are no longer aligned. Your soul is redirecting you.

It's uncomfortable and scares the crap out of most of us since feeling good is foreign. You have a passionate fire inside of you. Do not let others put it out. Also, do not judge others. It's vital right now to keep your heart activated and alive with courage, love, and laughter for you. There is not one thing I can't laugh at on this planet, even if it's me laughing at myself for missing a massive clue about something I didn't know.

What will you choose: freedom or a stranger's dumpster/prison rules? I have friends who have defied every odd: from death's door to overnight healing, unable to walk to full-on running and climbing mountains, crying kids hating school to homeschooling creating happy children in love with learning, quitting a job of 25 years to trusting the universe to redirect to self-employment success. The list is endless. Labels, titles, careers, and singular vocations are gone. Just focus on your truth, blueprint, and completing your puzzle piece. That's it.

EXERCISES

1. Truth trumps trash. Close your eyes for a moment and ask yourself for the truth about one "fact" you've been told, but it feels false. Please write it down. You won't like it at first because you'll have to see how you've gone along with it. Now, "clean it up" by writing what you know is THE truth.

2. What imagined prison are you in that you have created to keep you safe instead of free? You must decide on a non-negotiable plan to exit this real or imagined jail (health, wealth, relationship, environment, etc.).

3. What changes do I seek from others to avoid facing the limits their presence imposes on my authenticity? What judgment do I fear, hindering my focus on what my soul craves?

BADASSERY EXTRA CREDIT TIP

What would you do if you felt no cage or rules?

23

GOD'S GLOW

...

Here's a mind-boggler: why do so few people question the grand "why"? Why are we here? Why do only a few individuals ponder this profound "why"? Why do we exist?

And if questioning our beliefs about higher power creates conflict, should we investigate the reasons behind it? It seems we've stumbled upon the one inquiry that contradicts the sacred doctrines of all religions. So why do we willingly embrace the bundle of sacrifice, hatred, and hardship? It contradicts the fundamental teachings of any religion to endorse hate and suffering. Have we indeed become so detached from God? Why would anyone say," Yes! Sign me up for sacrifice, hate, and suffering." Have we really gotten so disconnected from God?

Have we lost the concept of knowing God? God is light. It's often said that God's son, Jesus, was the light of God, a single spark. So are you.

Are we still in the dark about who and what God is? God is the pure essence of light. God is the main act, and we are each just a glimmer of God's divine brilliance, mini stars in the cosmic sky. Our souls already know how to walk like Christ, Buddha, Krishna, Muhammad, or any other deity.

Here's the kicker: stop believing in things you haven't experienced personally. Forget the labels, boxes, holy writings, or the people preaching from far-off lands. Your path is to uncover your unique God-given glow. Imagine it this way: you started as a spark of divine light and came down to this earthly realm.

Make God proud by shining like the sun, i.e., living your purpose fully illuminated. Someone once said, "Don't dim your light to fit in; shine so bright that others are inspired to do the same." When you glow God's light inside your body, your inner lighthouse will shine as an example for others to find their way to illuminate their best selves.

Your glow is the light of love for someone who will look for it in their darkest days. Your God glow shines light from inside you, not in external rooms, doctrines, and deities. Your divine radiance is like a beacon of love, a guiding star for those lost in the darkest nights. No need to search for light in external places; you're the source.

What is the definitive recipe for self-sabotage? It is giving your power away to any guru, belief system, or indoctrination that has seen better days. You're a spark of God's light, and your mission is to light up your soul, not to suffer in the shadows imprisoning you from your free will.

The emerging toxicity you witness is a gradual unveiling of deeply ingrained, programmed beliefs that have confined you to a box of fear, sickness, or other low-frequency notions. Your purpose isn't to overlook God's light but to amplify it! You're not here to ignore God within you. You're here to turn it up! You're here to be an example of the gifts you came to share with humanity.

Your warrior spirit may have talents to heal, create security or safety, or mother. Perhaps you came as a chef, gardener, or even an actual warrior. Whatever your gift is, live it and shine!

What if, for example, how you believe you are supposed to show up and shine doesn't match the rhetoric or belief you've been taught? For instance, why haven't women throughout history been in leadership positions in religious or holy "boxed" traditions?

Have you ever wondered how people honored God (or Higher Powers) before these organized belief systems existed? What about the peaceful societies pre-Christ, pre-Buddha, or pre-Allah? Why not ask the questions that expand your soul? The above-mentioned spiritual giants were profound, but their real lessons were to help you see your own light.

You know what happened? We got complacent. We stopped asking "why" and started to believe in nonsense that made God feel far away, up in the clouds. Being told what to believe was easier than asking why. We accepted and were brainwashed by the external preachers over our internal intuition of love. We assumed it was okay, safe even, to not ask why. We were taught to believe that God was outside of us. As we all know, only a woman can create and carry a spark of light in her womb, yet in most religions, she is seen as less than to keep her power dimmed.

My point is not about gender. It's about not questioning why we accept that we're somehow less than God's radiant glow. Our true brilliance shines when we stop begging for salvation from a boxed belief system and embrace our superpowers of light!

EXERCISES

1. What is your spiritual or religious belief?

2. How would you respond if you found out some or all of your beliefs had been manipulated to keep you in a lack mindset?

3. Can you open your mind to God Consciousness over Indoctrinated Orders?

BADASSERY EXTRA CREDIT TIP

Discovering and embracing the divine essence within you and fully activating its potential, how would it impact your everyday existence?

24

LABELS LIMIT SO LOSE THEM

...

This will be my shortest chapter because it's the most straightforward truth to teach. Labels are losing options, so don't accept them. Ever. Here's what I mean.

For most of my life, I have been asked, as we all have been at one time or another, about what I do. Typically, the conversations sound something like this. I reply, "I validate truth."

"How do you do that? Are you a teacher, therapist, astrologer, coach, trainer, or author?"

"Ummmm…No. I raise self-worth, and how you find it from being in my presence is irrelevant as long as you feel it."

Every time you label yourself good or bad, you already lose because you force yourself onto a one-way road.

The moment you say, "I am losing, failing, fat, fearful, a disappointment, depressed, dumb, disabled, diseased, or dying," or any other low-frequency label, you will seek out every opportunity to validate those labels. You may be in a funk in some way at the moment but seek solutions for who you want to be. This is the easiest and fastest way to get out of your funk and feel free.

Why wouldn't strong, confident labels be a logical alternative? Imagine a CEO who only identifies as a business leader and exclusively handles tasks related to that role. What if that CEO might desire different exciting experiences that don't fit the CEO label? This CEO might avoid seeking out preferred or other environments or experiences just because of that title or label. It's better to remember that it's easier to see how you want to express yourself instead of how you want others to "feel" in your presence. If you want others to feel your leadership and guidance, incorporate these qualities into every aspect of your life. How you handle anyone "thing" is how you'll convey that feeling in "every" thing you do.

Ultimately, everyone's goal is to feel free of labels and limitations and be our authentic selves. Just choose the healthiest and highest frequency of yourself physically, mentally, and spiritually. No labels are needed.

This would look like… being your authentic self in every environment.

EXERCISES

1. What labels (positive and negative) do you use for yourself?

2. How do those labels limit you from expanding your gifts into more arenas?

3. What would you like others to feel from your presence in every room you enter?

4. Challenge yourself to see if you can stay in a state of authenticity in all environments you are in. Can you just be you without a mask?

BADASSERY EXTRA CREDIT TIP

What energy do you find easiest to shine in?
Can you shine that gift in every aspect of your life?

Conclusion

Embracing Your Inner Badassery

As we conclude this transformative journey, it's essential to reflect on the powerful insights and lessons we've explored throughout the chapters. This book has not been a typical self-help guide; it's a call to action, a challenge to confront and embrace your authentic self, and a guide to mastering the art of badassery in your life.

1. Self-Realization and Authenticity: From the very first chapter, "Who's the Boss of You?", we embarked on a quest for self-realization. This journey has been about understanding that you are in control of your life, your decisions, and your happiness. It's about rejecting the notion that others hold the keys to your fulfillment.

2. Confronting and Healing Inner Wounds: In chapters like "Expecting Wounded Souls to Save Us" and "Pain Is Your Internal Healer," we delved into the

importance of acknowledging and healing our inner wounds. We learned that pain, often avoided, is actually a crucial element in our personal growth and healing process.

3. Breaking Free from Limitations: "No More Effing Rules" and "Drama Stew" encouraged us to break free from societal norms and self-imposed limitations. The essence of badassery is about defying the odds, challenging the status quo, and living life on your own terms.

4. Emotional Intelligence and Awareness: In chapters like "Low Vibe Emotions" and "Truth Consciousness," we explored the significance of emotional intelligence. Understanding and managing our emotions is key to living a balanced and authentic life.

5. Relationships as Mirrors: "Relationships Are Revealing You" and "Your Parents' Marriage Mirage" taught us that our relationships are reflections of our

inner state. They challenge us to grow and provide opportunities for self-discovery and truth.

6. Spiritual and Personal Awakening: "Awakening is a Choice, Not an Event" and "God's Glow" emphasized the continuous nature of spiritual and personal awakening. It's a choice we make every day to live in our truth and connect with our higher selves.

7. The Power of Intention and Action: "Intentionally Burning Intentions?" and "Power Tools Come in Many Forms" highlighted the power of intention and action. It's not just about setting goals but also about taking consistent, purposeful actions towards achieving them.

8. Embracing the Journey: Finally, "Rat Race Realization" and "Astrology Lost Its Woo Woo" reminded us that this journey is unique for each individual. It's about embracing your path, learning

from your experiences, and growing to your fullest potential.

In essence, this book has been a guide to understanding and embracing your inner badass – that part of you that is unapologetically authentic, fiercely courageous, and relentlessly committed to personal growth and truth. It's about shedding the layers of societal expectations and self-doubt to reveal the powerful, confident individual you truly are. As you move forward, remember that badassery is not a destination but a continuous journey of self-discovery and empowerment. Keep challenging yourself, keep growing, and most importantly, keep shining your unique light in this world.

Thank you for embarking on this journey of mastering badassery with truth. May you continue to live boldly, love fiercely, and be the badass you are meant to be. Wishing you the life you truly deserve,
Daune

Journal Spot

This journal section is provided to capture your ADDITIONAL ah-ha! moments. There is no right or wrong way to use this section. Just keep all of your new positive, motivational, inspiring guidance here. This section can be whatever you make it, but remember, no rules. A grocery list, an affirmation that sings to you, a reminder to get dry cleaning, or just a place to express yourself.

JOURNAL SPOT

Mastering Badassery with Truth

EXPANSION PAGES

ALL EXPANSION PAGES ARE

PRINTABLE ONLINE

https://ideserveitnow.com/expansion-pdf-mastering-badassery/

CHAPTER 3

The liver flush link on the TOOLS page below.

https://ideserveitnow.com/dmts-book-suggestions

LOVE WATER

Link below for instructions

: https://ideserveitnow.com/love-water

CHAPTER 4

WINNING WHEEL

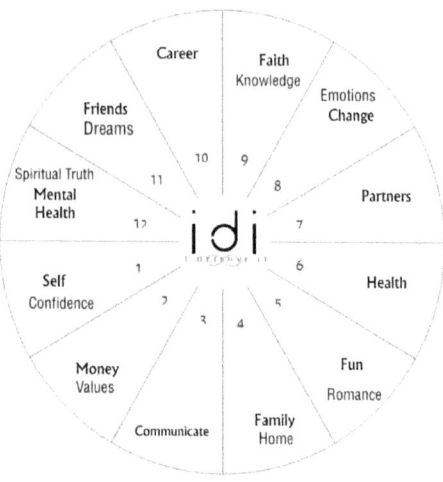

CHAPTER 5

PAIN PILLARS
IDESERVEITNOW.COM©

Safety
Sadness
Shame
Fear
Guilt
Trust

CHAPTER 8

Release & Renew (R & R)

Repeat R&R daily in your head & heart to interrupt emotional or physical pain imbalances.
(This healing tool works best when it is repeated daily up to 2-3X per day. The intention to heal is the key to healing!)

I ask Spirit to locate all known and unknown memories, feelings, beliefs, cellular memories and physical issues of _____ [your challenge or issue] at their original source.

Reveal each and every layer of this vibrational imbalance at its source. Review, open and heal it perfectly with Divine healing white light.

I allow it to be cleared through all directions of time and space, healing every aspect associated with it based on its origin at the cellular level. I forgive myself for every incorrect thought and forgive every person, place, circumstance, and event which contributed to this imbalanced thought process.

I give thanks for this awareness and now ask that every part of this energy be healed with unconditional love and forgiveness and ask the healing to be magnified by 100 times or more. I allow every layer of this vibrational pattern in physical, mental, emotional, spiritual or undesired behavior that is recorded poorly in any of my DNA blueprints to be released and transform to healthy state.

(Choose a new intention to replace old one & then hold a magnet or just your hand for convenience over your X Root of Spine, X Heart & X Crown of head while repeating empowered words [of 5 min].) I am [8] (empowered words). I Deserve [8].

I give thanks that... I Feel [8] (empowered words). I am [8] . I Deserve [8].

idi

deservetnow.com   Dawne Thompson

CHAPTER 9

Shower Talk

Release — Replace — Renew ☺

Speak to pain:

I cancel (insert) I no longer believe in that (insert).
I am no longer affected by that. It is the result of a
believe system, and I have the power to cancel it.
I don't have to accept that. I have the power to
sledgehammer and burn that belief.
I mean, this is ridiculous. I am an infinite being and
I love myself unconditionally.

Open Mind Consulting
info@idealercenzena.com

PRINTABLE **shower talk pdf** online

CHAPTER 16

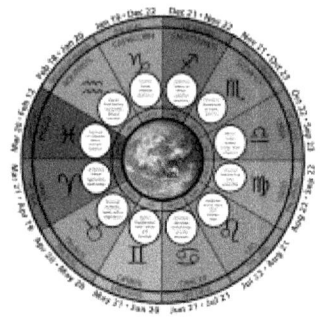

PRINT FREE BIRTH CHART

COURSE

ZODIAC WHEEL IS YOUR MEDICINE WHEEL

LEARN MORE ONLINE

https://ideserveitnow.com/idi-courses/

CHAPTER 17

LOVE WATER

Follow below for instructions.

https://ideserveitnow.com/love-water

CHAPTER 13

Print and learn the Zodiac Birth Chart

&

Print The Winning Wheel

Evaluate what areas of your life need attention.

FREE BIRTH CHART, LOCATED ON WEBSITE FOR PRINT:

ideserveitnow.com >> TOOLS

CHAPTER 19

Print and learn the Zodiac Birth Chart

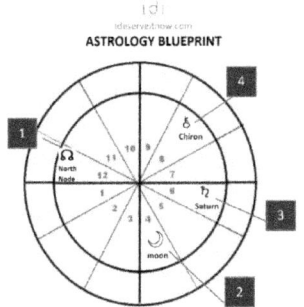

Look for Saturn & Moon descriptions.

See if these two areas of your life need attention.

(FREE BIRTH CHART)

ideserveitnow.com/free-birth-chart/HERE

CHAPTER 21

Print Marriage Mission on Expansion Page
(use for marriage, dating, or singles to create clarity)
Activity Click Below:

Marriage Mission

Creating a power couple relationship starts at the end.

Couples often start relationships with what they were taught from their parents and rarely begin with what they REALLY want to create as a team.

They are then shocked when they end up on different paths that pull them apart instead of together.

What kind of relationship do you want? Even if you are not married, you must decide the end destination you want. This is the biggest mistake even healthy couples make. Both focused on the same vision is powerful.
Be Clear, Concise & Specific.

List the end vision and characteristics of your ideal relationship.

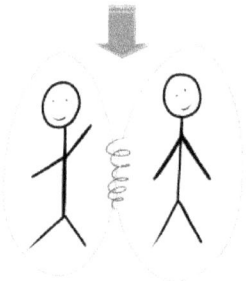

Write your end marriage mission here:
(Describe it in 10 Words or Less)

Open Mind Consulting
www.ideserveitow.com

CHAPTER 21

Each partner Print this and List 100 Characteristics of your
Ideal Mate/Relationship

Open Mind Consulting
www.ideserveitow.com

Resource Directory

idi Personal Success Coaching

"I see what you can't see." As a coach, Daune is powerful and direct in her ability to liberate people from their limitations and fears by showing them how to see truth in all aspects of their lives. She is on a mission to raise self-worth. More info: **ideserveitnow.com**

TRUTH WARRIOR SERIES Deep Dive Success Coaching

How you react to relationships with others, whether your *business partners, personal partners, parents, siblings, or children* can reveal profound truths about your actual capacity for success in all areas. All work and no play make for imbalance, but Daune has created a coaching system for achievement in both. **ideserveitnow.com/truth-warrior-training**

Warrior Pass Membership

Our all-access Warrior Pass is for winners who just want more and are willing to go get it. We're pretty sure you like the easy button as much as we do. Go ahead. Say it! I'm done playing small. Sign me up today. **ideserveitnow.com/idi-center-memberships**

Truth Tribe Membership
Explore the Universe and Learn to See the Unseen. The path toward happiness begins with speaking our truth. Sometimes, this involves letting go of things that don't serve our purpose. Join Daune free for Live Q&A.
ideserveitnow.com/idi-center-memberships/

I Deserve Apparel
Unleash your confidence and style with these incredible threads. Feel the cozy embrace that screams, "I am unstoppable!" Our shirts and hoodies are more than mere garments. They are motivation machines, radiating vibrant energy and love wherever you go. Modern designs to proudly embody 100% badassery. So go ahead, let your inner BADASS shine, and showcase your unique style to the world.
ideserveitapparel.com

Spotify & Apple Podcast
Visit Daune for your daily dose of Truth.
Truth Tribe -Daune Thompson

www.ideserveitnow.com
info@ideserveitnow.com
Scottsdale, AZ 85258

About the Author

Daune Thompson

Daune currently resides in Scottsdale, AZ., with her husband Tony.

Daune holds a bachelor's degree in Kinesiology and is a Certified Life Coach. She has an extensive fitness background and has taught at the University of Wisconsin-Milwaukee and Dow Chemical. Following an extensive fitness career, Daune became Director of Training and Development for a national speaker's bureau while developing training programs and customizing employee-relations courses for Fortune 500 companies (i.e., Kimberly Clark Corp., Menasha Corp., etc.).

Daune's entrepreneurial talent includes successfully owning and operating businesses in the beauty, wellness, and self-help industries. While she owned Salon Dor hair salon, she developed programs designed to build confidence from the inside out. She has authored several self-empowerment journals and books including, the *I Deserve It manual*, *Drama Detox* and *Balls - Building Balanced Relationships* to name a few.

As a coach, Daune is powerful and direct in her ability to liberate people from their limitations and fears. Daune's coaching talents focus on relationships, life purpose, and personal and professional growth. She is on a mission to raise the self-worth of others by guiding them to create balance, clarity, and success in their lives.

Daune conducts personal coaching for clients across the country and facilitates "I Deserve it Self-Mastery" courses and seminars monthly. She empowers individuals daily to remove roadblocks that hinder them from their greatest potential, encouraging them to live the life they Deserve.

www.ingramcontent.com/pod-product-compliance
Lightning Source LLC
Chambersburg PA
CBHW070138100426
42743CB00013B/2749